ANGEL WHISPERS

A Journey into the World of the Earth's Oldest Guardians

Angel Hugs + Love

Morgana Starr

2011

Copyright © 2011 Morgana Starr

ISBN 978-1-61434-524-4

All rights reserved. No part of this publication may be reproduced, stored in a retrieval system, or transmitted in any form or by any means, electronic, mechanical, recording or otherwise, without the prior written permission of the author.

Published in the United States by Booklocker.com, Inc., Bangor, Maine.

Printed in the United States of America on acid-free paper.

Booklocker.com, Inc.
2011

First Edition

Artistic Designer of Anael's Symbol
Shandie Savage
psychekitty@yahoo.com

Graphic Design of Anael's Symbol
Amanda Wyatt of Wyatt Graphic Designs
www.wyattgraphicdesigns.com

Edited by Betsy Shanahan of Orlando, Florida
Freelance Editor
betsy@betsyshanahan.com.

ANGEL WHISPERS

A Journey into the World of the Earth's Oldest Guardians

By
Morgana Starr

TABLE OF CONTENTS

DEDICATION vii
ACKNOWLEDGEMENTS viii
ANAEL'S SYMBOL 1
THE UNIVERSE MADE CONSCIOUS..................................... 2
ANGELIC BEINGS 8
PARABLES 11
    PARK BENCH ANGEL 13
    ANGELIC QUILT 27
    ANGELIC ASSISTANCE 29
    THANKS-GIVING 31
    POPSICLE ANGEL 34
    LET GO 36
ANGEL WHISPERS 39
ANGELIC ENCOUNTERS 166
    ANGELS WALK AMONG US 167
    ANGEL MECHANICS 169
    DAD'S ANGEL 170
    HOSPITAL ANGEL 171
    SURGEON'S ANGEL 172
    ANGEL DOODLING MESSAGE 174
    GUARDIAN LAUNDRY ANGEL 176
    SHIELDING WITH ANGEL LOVE 178
    ANGEL DRAGONS 180
MESSAGES FROM ANGELS 185
    An Angel called White Feather 187
    Shandie's Angel 189
    Cynthia's Angel 190
    Archangel Azrael 192
    Archangel Sariel 199
    Wendy's Angel 202
    Jenni's Angel 204
    Angels of the Violet Ray 205
    An Angel called Rose 207
    Archangel Azrael 209

Various Archangels	212
An Angel called Az	217
PROTECTION, HEALING AND CLEARING MEDITATION	229
FINAL WORDS FROM ANAEL	231
ABOUT THE AUTHOR	233
CONTRIBUTING AUTHORS	235

DEDICATION

This book is dedicated to all my 'Angels'. As my life and even my physical appearance transformed, you asked me to share with you my secret. I began teaching the modalities given to me by the angel, Anael, which facilitated my change.

My greatest joy has been as I have watched my clients become empowered with this angelic energy. You are my inspiration for continuing the work set out for me by the angels.

Then many of you began to ask for more information about this beautiful Divine angel.

This propelled me to write the first of her books to share this message of unconditional love, hope and unity.

My clients have become my friends and partners in this Angelic Mission. I am very blessed.

The following Angel Whisper is for you, my dear 'Angels'

'Sunshine and joy you bring to me each day,
Brightening my life in your own special way.
Sunbeam rays straight from your heart do come,
Now I know where the sparkling rainbows are from.'

ACKNOWLEDGEMENTS

I want to thank the angels, especially Anael, who gave me the strength and hope to shift my life into the beautiful space in which I now live.

My soul has no words to express my appreciation to Tim Tedana, my dear friend and confidant. He has brought balance and true unconditional love to my life creating a haven for my heart sing and my spirit to be safe. This enabled my wings to unfurl, soar with the angels and be of better service to humanity.

Many thanks to my dear friend, Cheryl (Lilianna) Kaldahl, whose emotional support, love and friendship through many lifetimes encouraged me to keep going during the hard times.

I am forever grateful to my friend and mentor, Andrea de Michaelis, whom has encouraged my spiritual growth by her kind words and guidance. She walks her talk in a beautiful example of love with no judgments or ego attached.

There are so many more to thank that it would fill the pages of another book. Suffice to say that all of you whom have touched my life have also touched my heart. You are all a valuable part of this angelic mission of love and unity.

ANAEL'S SYMBOL

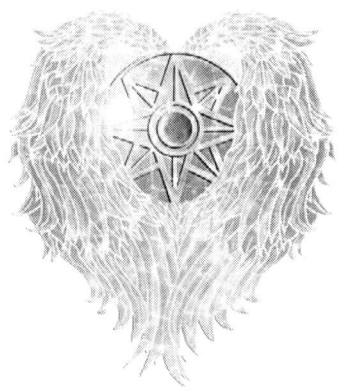

All angels have symbols. This is Anael's symbol. Here is the description of what it means.

The center of the symbol represents the individual. The circle surrounding the center is the community connected with the individual. The points of the star that go straight up, down and to either side represent the four directions of the earth (North, South, East and West) and all spiritual energies associated with each direction. The other four points represent the elements of air, water, fire and earth.

The outer circle is representative of Divine Spirit that unites the individual, the community, all of the elements and directions into a beautiful space of Unconditional Love. The wings represent the angels as helpers of the Divine, enfolding all in a space of Unconditional Love, Power and Healing.

THE UNIVERSE MADE CONSCIOUS

Anael is the Archangel of Love and Princess over the other angels. She can call in whichever angel or angels are needed for your particular issue. In many texts you will see Anael being depicted as a male. Of course, angels are androgynous (neither male nor female). Anael has taken a feminine form in imparting information to Morgana, as Anael says is necessary to bring feminine balance back to the world.

Anael carries the essence of the Feminine Divine, the Mother aspect of God. She is like the fierce tiger protecting her young and the gentle duck encompassing her fledglings in wings of love and comfort.

Her message is one of unconditional love, forgiveness and empowerment. That means drawing boundaries… not allowing anyone to take your energy. She helps to reawaken the human race with the gifts given to them by the Divine.

Here is her story in her own words:

We angels were here at the beginning of time. When I came into consciousness, there was only Darkness around me. I reached out with my being and felt the essence of the Divine One who had created me. I experienced the incredible Love and Oneness as I merged with the Divine. The darkness was comfortable and a part of me, however I felt something was missing. There was no balance…only darkness…though in the darkness I could still feel the Divine One within me.

The Divine One had first brought Light into my essence, so I became an embodiment of Light. As one of the Divine's first creations, I was given the gift of being able to ignite a Divine spark of Light within each and every new being that was created. It was a great responsibility and a great honor.

Then the Divine One created more Angels and put sparks of Light within them. I was given the ability to create also, as I was created in His image. I created Angels with special Sparks of Light within them. These would be my helpers and companions in spreading Light through dark places that needed illumination. These Angels of Light I created for a Divine purpose. I named them the Elohim.

When the Divine decided to create a new world, I was honored by being one of the chosen ones to assist to bring Light into the darkness. This was because I was one of the first to have the experience of Light. For without Light, the beings that were to be created to live on this world would exist in a place full of turmoil and fear.

Beauty on so many levels was unveiled as Light flowed through the darkness. There was only enough Light allowed to bring balance. If too much Light was brought into the darkness, the new beings would be blinded. The balance allowed for shadows to play around the corners and edges of the new creations. The Light flowed across the new world as it was called into existence.

I gasped in wonder as the Light across the sky of this world exploded into rainbows of exquisite color! The beauty in the bending and blending of light and color showed to me the power in merging diverse energies into a united whole.

All the angels watched with interest as the Divine One brought the rest of creation into life. When humans were created, we felt joy flood our spirits as a deep love for the human race was awakened within us. They were amazing, with gifts and abilities that held no boundaries except those they set for themselves.

Imagine our thrill when we were given the task of working directly with our beloved humans. We were to watch and give messages to people, helping them move ahead in their lives. We unveiled for them their ability to activate those gifts and abilities.

When humans made the decision that they wanted to understand good from evil, the Divine gave them the gift of free will. Many of us angels were excited, knowing their lives would then have richness in it that would have otherwise been vacant.

However, there were some angels that felt jealous. They thought the Divine loved humans more than them. That made them angry. Their anger turned inward and it dampened their inner spark of Light. They were consumed with darkness. They made it their task to bring their darkness into the lives of humans. They felt that if they made life hard for humans, that the humans would curse the Divine One that created them. Then the Divine One would no longer love the humans, but would love the angels more.

These angels manipulated and blocked the Light from humans. They encouraged humans to stop thinking for themselves, but to go with the thoughts of one or two humans without questioning. The humans that listened to these angels became like confused sheep following a lost shepherd.

I and my angels of Light began our tireless work of helping humankind. We needed to understand what humans went through in order to assist them more efficiently. Our love for humans was so intense we were willing to walk in this earthly life, giving up the etheric realm. Some of us chose to take human bodies at various times throughout the history of this earth. This would be a body in which the human soul abdicated because life was going to be too hard. So when we took a body, we took on the Karmic debt of the body. This we did gladly, so by going through the human experience we were better able to understand, thereby better able to assist humans in their growth.

Those angels are what are known as embodied angels. They took human families and experienced deep sadness and joy. They understand the pain of betrayal as well as the joy of being enfolded in a loved one's embrace. When their human body would sleep, their angel essence could travel freely. Then they would report back to the other angels that watch over you and explain the issues of being human.

This earth plane is like a school yard. Humans are here to learn different lessons. You choose these lessons while in heaven. In one life you may have the experience of being very wealthy and treating those around you poorly. In the next lifetime that you are here you choose to have the understanding of poverty, having rich people look down upon you. Each lifetime builds upon the next.

We angels have been at your side each lifetime, whispering messages of hope and enlightenment in your ears. We do not perform miracles. That is something that you have the capacity to do. Our job is to help you see that by being made in the image of the Divine, you can become your own creators. Thereby you can make whatever reality you wish come into existence by your mere thought and intent. The only boundaries that exist are the ones you set for yourself.

We are with you and want to help you in every aspect of your lives. Some compare themselves and their pain to what others go through. They feel that they should not ask the angels or the Divine for help, as someone else's pain may be greater than theirs may.

However, another person's pain does not diminish yours. Remember pain is here to teach you. The lesson you must learn from your pain is something that only you can unveil. By giving up your control to the angels of the Divine and asking for assistance, you acknowledge that you are ready to learn the lesson.

This is your first step in releasing the pain. You will be better able to walk through the pain, learn the lesson and thereby release it, if you call on the angels for help. Remember always that we are ready to assist and are honored to serve.

Stepping on the stones as you cross the rushing river of life must be done with trust in the Divine if they are to be traversed in safety. In order to take another step forward, one foot must leave the apparent security of a stone to move onto another. There is a moment when only one foot is touching a stone and the other is hovering in mid-air. For many, this is a frightening time. For those who know their outstretched hands are held and supported by their angel, they can easily take that step in confidence and eventually dance across the river.

For those who want to maintain control they are frozen in place, unable to take another step while they wistfully watch their friends 'dance' across the river of life. I encourage you to 'let go', connect with the angels and join me in the 'joyful dance of life'.

In addition, we angels are here to teach you about healing. We are here to assist you in your healing. Being in physical bodies, your first thought about healing is in relationship to your physical bodies. However, until you have stepped into a space of Divine energy bringing healing to your spirits, you cannot totally heal on the physical level.

Remember that you are embodied eternal universal energy that has the ability to constantly recreate a new physical body. If you recreate the same dis-ease in your body, then you have not yet learned the lesson that is within that dis-ease. Some of this comes because you must release negative thought patterns and belief systems that have been programmed into you from an early age.

When you ask us to assist in healing of your dis-ease, we will guide you with ideas and questions to encourage you to discover the answer for yourself. This is how we work with you who are at an advanced level. You hear us and translate the thoughts into words to assist those others whose vibration is not at a level to hear us.

The most important thing for us to do is to teach about unconditional love. We use our energies to "rise above" the hate and misconceptions and love people in their ignorance. We teach you how to join us in that flight of freedom and joy.

Unconditional Love is letting go of control. One must let go of control and let each person follow their own path. Allow them to dance their own dance.

When you love someone regardless of their feelings for you and regardless of what they choose to do with their life, you have taken the step towards unconditional love. Think about how many times you have told someone, "I love you no matter what, I just want you to be happy." You think you are showing unconditional love. However, as soon as you say, "I just want you to be happy" you put conditions on your love.

You must be able to say, "I love you not matter what, whether you are happy or sad, rich or poor, like me or hate me. I simply love you." Being attached to their reactions to you causes you to step back into control, thereby getting off the track of unconditional love.

This is hardest to do with family. We think we know what is best for them and try to control them by telling them we just want them to be happy. Instead, just love them with no judgments on the path they choose to walk. It is their journey and their lesson. Why would you want to take that from them?

Speaking of family, they may choose not to love you in the same way. Allow them that space and then perhaps you may find it is healthier for you to put some distance between them and you. After all you chose to have them as your blood family to learn lessons of life.

The exciting part of life right now is that your soul family is gathering! Those you have been with in other lifetimes and done much healing and spiritual work are beginning to find you. You will feel closer to them than any blood related ties. Remember with them also to show this beautiful unconditional love. This will make your connection stronger as you unite on a mission of service to mankind.

Don't forget to keep the balance in all things. Laugh and enjoy your life experiences. Your biggest 'job' here is the pursuit of happiness and adventure with its own unique perspective.

~ARCHANGEL ANAEL~

ANGELIC BEINGS

Angels take many different forms depending on what you are comfortable with. Perhaps one might appear as the typical warrior with wings (if you were looking for protection) or as a beautiful lady in a gauzy robe with wings (if you were looking for comfort). Your angel could appear as an animal: buffalo, horse, dragon, griffon, or even a kitten! It is formed from what you perceive to be protective, healing and of the Light.

If you want to know your particular angel's name, just ask. When a name pops into your head -- that is your angel's name. If not, then pick a name. Names aren't important to them. Most will choose the name of someone familiar who has crossed over because you already have a connection to that name. The comfort of someone who knows your heart is familiar and you have already built trust with them.

We have different angels for different situations. Your guardian angel - everyone is assigned at least one - will help you without you asking at perilous times. Such as the stories you have heard about an angel pulling someone from a wrecked car.

However, the angels not assigned to you are different. They will help you when you ask. They watch and wait for you to ask them for help. By asking, you make available to you the hosts of heaven. Don't forget to THANK Them!

Archangel Michael - protector and warrior; Archangel Gabrielle - creative expression, music and writing; Archangel Raphael - healing of mind and body, to name a few. There are several books out about the different energies of the angels and how to work with them, so I will not focus on that here.

When you call on Anael she can send out to you whatever angel you need. It is like calling someone that can delegate to you the energies that you need, when and how you need it.

This saves you from learning all the particularities of each angel, though knowing in general can be helpful.

So many people are affected by the negativity around them. With Anael's help you can protect yourself from those energies as well as heal yourself. This is done by accessing the inherent gifts of the Divine.

She wants to empower us with those gifts. These are gifts of healing, inner (psychic) sight and astral travel to name only a few. Jesus said, "These things I do, you too will do, and more!" Look at what He did. He us left with the promise that we could do more than He did!

Anael is here to help us accomplish that. When we activate our inner sight we are activating our greatest gift given to us as a child. Jesus said, "Unless we become as children, we will not inherit the kingdom of Heaven!"

By using these gifts, we transcend and transform even our physical bodies and bring Heaven into our hearts and lives!

PARABLES

Channeled by

Morgana Starr

PARK BENCH ANGEL

Helen walked down the sidewalk, her heart heavy with despair. Her baggy clothes hung loosely on her body and she hid her unruly hair under a ball cap. The depression that came from being unable to find a job had taken its toll on her body. Every bone in her body ached. She was too young to have such aches and pains. Her mom told it was the beginning of arthritis. "That doesn't make sense," Helen thought to herself, "I'm only 34!"

Walks through the park usually helped to clear her head and lighten her spirit, but lately she was just going through the motions. Why she even bothered to come to the park today, she had no idea. But something was urging her and, in spite of the pain in her body, she found herself walking down the twisting pathway.

She came to the familiar bench where she often sat to ponder her fate in life. As she lowered herself down, she sensed something was different this day. It was as if there was a feeling of joy around the bench. She shook her head. This depression had affected her senses, she thought. Maybe any place other than her own house would feel better, since that is where she spent most of her time.

She reviewed in her mind the talk she had with her friend, Maria. Last night, Maria had said, "In order to help yourself, you need to ask for help from the Angels. They will help you, if only you ask."

Helen had answered, "I don't believe angels are here for that. I am not sure that I even believe in God!"

"Okay, Helen. Just remember what I said. What can it hurt?" Maria replied.

As Helen thought about the conversation, the words "Why not ask? What can it hurt?" came into her head. I have tried about everything else and I am not getting anywhere, she thought.

In spite of someone possibly overhearing her, though no one was in sight, Helen took a deep breath and said aloud, "Okay Maria's angels -- I need some help. Will you please help me get a job I enjoy, one that pays well and also, can you help me get out of this pain and depression?"

"Well, the first thing you need to do is to not take yourself too seriously," came a deep voice directly beside her.

Helen jumped at the sound! She turned her head and seated on the bench next to her was a well dressed gentleman.

"I...I...didn't see you sitting there! Did you just get here?" Helen asked. Confusion was obvious in her voice.

A hardy chuckle escaped his lips. "I have been here for quite some time. You were so absorbed in yourself that you didn't see me sitting here when you sat down."

Helen found herself facing an impeccably groomed middle-aged man. He looked like he should be sitting behind a desk on Wall Street instead of a park bench in a small neighborhood. There was a hint of gray at the temples of his finely sculpted black hair, giving him a sophisticated air of wisdom. A twinkle in his steel grey eyes hinted at a sense of humor behind his polished façade. He had a look of wisdom that was not constrained by his age.

As his mouth turned upwards in a grin, Helen realized she had been caught in the act of staring. She blushed profusely and stuttered, "I...I...am so sorry. You caught me by surprise, I apologize for staring. You must think I'm rude."

That brought a hardy laugh from him. "I don't think you're rude, Helen. Your heart is too kind for rudeness to live there," he responded.

"How do you know my name? How can you know anything about me?" Helen was feeling a bit nervous now as she wondered how this man knew her.

The twinkle in his eyes appeared again as he responded, "I come to this park a lot and I've seen you out there." He gestured towards an open area close by. "You feed the squirrels and I've overheard you talk to them. You usually say something like, 'hi, it's me, Helen. Remember, I won't hurt you. I just want to feed you.'"

Helen relaxed as she knew that was almost a daily practice with her. She had gotten so comfortable doing it that she no longer looked around to see if anyone was watching her. There also was something about him that reminded her of her father, making her feel more comfortable.

"What is your name, since you know mine now?" she said with a smile, looking up into his face.

"Harold. Yes, I know it is old fashioned," he said when he noticed her questioning look. "But that's me; I was raised on chivalry and all that stuff."

"Oh, well it's a nice name," she answered. "Why do you come to the park, Harold?"

"I thought that would be obvious by the way I'm dressed," he answered.

As Helen continued to look puzzled, the man continued, "I have a high-stress job. I come here to connect with nature and be around other people doing the same. It helps me unwind."

The answer set Helen at ease. "I know what you mean. I not only need to unwind, but I need direction right now. I was hoping by coming here today and by relaxing, somehow I could get some clarity."

"What is it that you need clarity with?" was Harold's response.

Helen found herself relating to him some of the challenges in her life that had brought her to where she found herself now. "I just don't like the way I feel," she said. "Some days I can hardly get out of bed in the mornings. I would like to just sleep and let everything go away. But I know that isn't the answer. I just want to feel better," she concluded as tears streamed down her face.

A white handkerchief was gently put in her hand and without a thought to her embarrassment; Helen wiped her damp face and loudly blew her nose.

"Thank you, I'll wash it and bring it back to you," she said.

Harold chuckled, "That's okay. Keep it. There may be a time when you'll need it for someone else's tears. But right now let's begin to help you."

"What do you mean?" Helen asked.

"That's what I do. I'm an empowerment coach. I assist people at taking power back in their lives," was Harold's answer.

"That is awesome, but I can't pay you, Harold. I don't have a job. I'm so behind in bills that it's going to take me a long time to catch up," replied Helen, sadly.

"Then this is your lucky day! Every month I take on a client per-gratis. It's my way to give back to the world. I haven't picked my client for this month, so if you're willing to shift some of your realities, you can be that person. It won't be easy. I'm going to ask you to shift some of your belief systems and way of talking, but I can help you create a new reality for yourself." Harold asked, "Are you game?"

Helen's eyes grew wider with each word out of Harold's mouth. The miracle she needed might be right in front of her! Was she game? She would be crazy to say 'no'. She was at the bottom of her life; why not give it a try?

"Sure! I'm ready for a change. Thank you so much!" Helen said hopefully.

"First of all, I want you to understand that you can create the reality you wish by simply changing the way you think and speak, little one," came his gentle response.

"I don't know how to do that," Helen stated.

"I know, and I will help you with that." Harold smiled in a way that gave her confidence. He continued, "I will be giving you an assignment every day. It's important that you do each assignment. I'll meet you here regularly so we can review and I'll give you something new to work on. Does that sound okay?"

"Certainly," Helen answered. Hope was beginning to flood through her. Something deep within was telling her that this was a pivotal time in her life.

"Assignment Number One: You will write out affirmations and post them around your home. Put them at eye level. Here are some examples: 'I am a wonderful person.' 'Positive people love to be around me.' 'I have a well paying job that I enjoy.' 'My body is healthy and strong.' 'I have more money than I need.' These affirmations will work on your subconscious to shift your conscious life," Harold said.

"I'll do that right away. But what about a job? I need a job right now!" Helen replied.

"I know of a job that would be perfect for you, but we have to make you perfect for the job. The only thing holding you back is how you feel about yourself. You aren't ready for this job yet. Here is the good news, though. If you do this work on yourself, you'll be ready very soon, I promise," Harold said with a reassuring smile.

"Also, here's an affirmation I want you to say -- with conviction -- every morning before you leave the house. I have it written out on this card. Copy it and put it on your bathroom mirror. Say it while you look at yourself in the mirror. Carry this card with you to pull out and say when you need it," Harold continued.

Helen took the proffered card and read:
All the glory I have inside
Comes to the surface and cannot hide
Everyone sees the love shining through
In everything I say and do
From this day forth through eternity
Prosperity, great health and love will come to me

"I will try," Helen said hesitantly.

Harold raised an eyebrow at her, looking almost stern. "Obviously we must practice. Listen to me, as I say it."

Harold repeated the words of the affirmation. As he spoke it seemed as if he began to glow with an inner light. When he finished, his broad smile brightened the whole area.

"Now you do it," Harold said with confidence.

"I'm sure I won't be able to say it as good as you can," Helen said.

"I'm not asking you to. I'm asking you to say it as good as YOU can," he said.

With a deep breath, Helen said, "Okay, here goes!" She then read the affirmation aloud.

When she looked at Harold for approval, he merely nodded his head and with a slight smile said, "Say it again. FEEL and MEAN what you say. You can do it!"

Since he sounded so confident, Helen tried again. A warm feeling of contentment and joy filled her. For just a moment she wondered where this was coming from but then she spoke the affirmation aloud again. This time she let go of feeling self-conscious. She lost herself in the words and felt the meaning behind them. When she finished, her whole body was buzzing with happiness. She looked up at Harold with radiant eyes.

"Now that was perfect! You have a sparkle in your eyes and your smile radiates a deep inner peace," Harold said. "I am very proud of you," he added.

For some reason that gave Helen even more joy. "Thank you, I feel better already!" she said enthusiastically.

"Of course you do. What you speak, you bring into your reality," he said. "Now I want you to go home and make a list of everything you want to have in your life. Bring it here tomorrow so we can work on it together. Be specific. Don't just ask for a job. Ask where, how much you want to be paid, how you want your co-workers to be, etcetera. But I want you do it in the following format; 'I am so happy and grateful now that I...' This is how you must begin each of the things you ask for. Claim it like it has already happened! For example: 'I am happy and grateful now that I have more money than I need!"

"That would be great. I could use some money right now!" Helen emphatically stated.

Harold smiled with a patient look on his face. "This is the beginning, Helen. Just do the work so you can begin to create the reality you want. I will look forward to seeing your list tomorrow."

"Thank you, so much. I'll do everything you said. It's strange, but I don't feel so depressed now," Helen replied as she got up and shook Harold's hand. A feeling of acceptance and peace flowed through her.

Amazed at the difference in her feelings, she turned to thank Harold again and was startled to see he was nowhere in sight! How could that be? There were only a few scattered trees near the park bench. He couldn't have disappeared into thin air, could he? Shaking her head in confusion, she returned home. She was acutely aware that the pain in her body was not as strong now as it had been earlier.

The next morning dawned bright and clear. Helen rushed to the park filled with excitement and anticipation. She had done the requested work and had her notebook firmly clutched in her hand.

Looking around for Harold to no avail, she seated herself on the bench and waited.

Excitement changed to worry as time passed and he failed to appear. Chaotic thoughts tumbled through her head. "He did say today, didn't he? Maybe he got frustrated with me and decided not to come. Maybe he had an appointment with his paying clients and felt I wasn't worth the trouble. I'm just a bother to a lot of people," Helen stated out loud with a deep sigh.

"Then obviously you've been hanging around the wrong kind of people," came a clearly male voice next to Helen.

"Oh, my gosh!" Helen jumped in her seat, visibly startled. "Where did you come from?" she asked Harold who was seated beside her on the bench.

"I walked up here a few minutes ago, but you were self-absorbed, so I was waiting for you to say something." Harold's smile was full of compassion. A peaceful calm washed over Helen. She handed him her notebook, opened to the affirmations she had written.

Taking the notebook from Helen, Harold slowly read through her affirmations. He took out his pen, crossed out a couple of words and added a few.

Harold chuckled with a smile on his face, "Take that frown off your face, little one. You look like you're afraid you're in trouble. Remember there is no right or wrong, just experiences, although some experiences are far more interesting than others!"

He concluded with a deep belly laugh. His laughter was so infectious that Helen began to laugh with him, effectively erasing all her stress and worry.

"I just fine tuned things a bit for you. I had forgotten to tell you that you should make sure that all affirmations avoid the use of words like "no, never, and such. So instead of 'I never get sick', you write 'I am always healthy'. The body responds to whatever words you say and brings that energy to you. Words are powerful. Thoughts, then written words and then spoken words are the order of power."

"Wow, I never thought of it that way, but it all makes sense," responded Helen.

"I want you to work with these affirmations in this way: say them aloud and often, every day. Say them with energy and excitement. Feel the emotion associated with each. This helps to shift your reality from future wishes into present reality. Any questions?"

"No, except, what is my next step after that?" Helen answered eagerly.

Harold laughed, "You are an eager one!"

"Well, I'm tired of where I've been. Since I met you yesterday, I feel better than I've felt in ages!" she responded.

"Okay, I'll give you the next assignment since you want to be on the 'fast track'.

You must keep your energy field protected. You strongly feel other people's emotions. It's important that you shift from experiencing their emotions to only sensing them, without it affecting you in a negative way. That's why you have so many aches and pains lately."

"How did you know that I've been hurting a lot recently?" Helen asked with a puzzled expression on her face.

"I've been doing this work for a long time. I see what other people do not," Harold clarified.

"I have written a meditation for you to do. This is done by calling on the angel Anael. She has given this modality to help the human race to empower them to more fully develop their spiritual gifts. She is an Archangel. That means she is kind of like a general in the angel world. Here it is. Read it aloud right now." Harold said firmly.

Helen took the paper and began to read the words feeling a beautiful sensation of joy and hope fill her as she read.

"Archangel Anael, please create a Divine pyramid of protection around me. The top of the pyramid is connected to the heart of the Divine where there is a valve leading inwards only. At the bottom in each corner are valves leading outwards only. Anything touching the bottom of the pyramid is instantly transmuted into love…siphoned to the corner valves sent into Mother Earth to balance and heal her.

It fills my pyramid, filtering through my body taking any negativity, worries or imbalances. This goes to the bottom of my pyramid being instantly transmuted into Love, through the valves to balance and heal Mother Earth.

Anael, please manifest a rainbow through my pyramid and through my body, balancing and healing each chakra. Please fill my pyramid with tiny rainbows full of joy!

Anything negative that brushes the sides of my pyramid and is instantly transmuted into love, great health and prosperity on every level for me.

Please cloak the outside of my pyramid, so darkness will not perceive my Light as I shine brighter and brighter on my Divine Path.

Anael, please keep the pyramid and rainbows with me always. Thank You, Anael for your help and assistance."

"Wow, I'm tingling from head to toe!" Helen joyfully exclaimed.

"That's because you are truly ready for a change in your life," answered Harold.

"Your homework is to read this once a day for a week. Every day pause three times a day and take three slow, deep breaths while thinking of this pyramid around you. As you think, so it is." He concluded with a smile.

"Okay, I'll do it!" Helen exclaimed excitedly.

"I know you will. I'll meet you here a week from today same time, same place."

This time, Helens' exuberance overcame her as she gave Harold a hug while blurting out, "Thank you sooo much!"

His smile was that of a doting older uncle. "You're welcome. Enjoy your week!"

As she walked off with a bounce in her step, she thought she should ask Harold his phone number. As she turned, confusion flooded over her. Where did he go? It was just like yesterday when he had disappeared into the proverbial thin air. Looking at her notebook where Harold had made his corrections helped her feel a bit better. It proved that he had really been there. For a moment she wondered if she had her lost grip on her sanity!

The week passed swiftly as she did the 'homework'. She continued to feel better and better. On the morning she was to meet Harold, she received a call to go to an interview for a job the next day!

Helen restrained herself from running to the park, anxious to tell Harold of her new job offer. Like the week before, he was nowhere in sight, so she sat on the bench and just waited. She pulled out her notebook and began saying her affirmations aloud.

"That sounds terrific!" Harold's familiar voice right next to her snapped her back to the here and now.

"You did it again!" she exclaimed, "You appeared out of nowhere!"

"It takes special eyes to see what is right in front of you, my little one," was his patient reply. "So tell me what you're so excited about."

Helen excitedly related to him the details of her new job offer. Harold reached out to shake her hand and said, "I am honored to meet the new Senior Councilor for Healing Humanity, Incorporated."

Helen shook his hand, but the confusion in her voice was evident as she asked, "But I don't have the job yet."

Harold looked at her a bit sternly and said, "That's just a matter of timing and creation. Tweak your affirmation to reflect you holding the position, such as, 'I am so happy and excited that I am now the Senior Councilor for Healing Humanity, Incorporated.'"

"Wow, that sounds great!" Helen exclaimed.

"There are few more things you can to do to make sure this job becomes a reality," Harold continued. He spent the next hour counseling and giving Helen direction as she scribbled every word furiously in her notebook.

The next week when they met again, Helen shared the news of the second interview. The following week she was hired as the new Senior Councilor for Healing Humanity, Incorporated.

"I am so proud of you, Helen, you have done great! You look professional and full of confidence," Harold said.

That's because of you and your help," she replied.

"You did the work, little one," was his response. "I merely offered assistance after you asked for help."

"What do you mean? You offered to help me," Helen was confused.

"Only after you asked." Harold said.

"I was blurting out about Maria's angels and asking them for help...." Helen paused and looked intently at Harold.

A bright glow began to appear around him. The air shimmered and a misty haze lifted from the ground. Straining her eyes, Helen struggled to make out Harold's form. She saw his shape grow and expand until her sight was filled with an angel more beautiful than she could have imagined even in her wildest dreams. His pearlescent wings glinted in the sun, scattering rainbows all around.

Harold smiled at her and said, "Angels appear in many forms. They will show themselves to you when you ask for their help, but in a form that makes you comfortable. You can create whatever you wish in your life by using the tools I gave you."

Tears flowed down Helen's face as she was overcome by the enormity of what had just happened. "What can I do to thank you?" she asked in an awestruck voice.

"I only ask that you freely share this information with whoever needs it," was Harold's reply. "And remember that we angels are here to help anytime, but we will not interfere. We only wait to be asked. Our love for you humans goes beyond the constraints of this earth."

A feeling of deep Unconditional Love washed over Helen, filling her eyes with tears.

Looking down she reached into her bag to pull out a tissue. After wiping her eyes and blowing her nose, she looked up to see Harold had disappeared.

This time she felt a deep sense of contentment and peace. She knew she was never alone. She had only to ask for help from the angels and help would appear, in one form or another. She chuckled softly to herself as she walked home.

Several weeks passed before Helen had an opportunity to visit the park again. She was dressed in a professional business suit. There was lightness in her step and she smiled, remembering how pain and depression were no longer a part of her life.

Walking past her favorite bench, she saw an older lady sitting there. The lady was dressed poorly, no makeup, with her hair pulled back under a hat. Her face revealed a trail of sparkling tears. Sitting next to her was an older man. He was scruffy in appearance. His clothes labeled him as a park maintenance man. They seemed to be engrossed in a deep discussion.

"You can create the reality you wish, by simply changing the way you think and speak, little one," came the man's soft words.

The familiar words stopped her in her tracks. The man paused in his speaking as she had halted just in front of him. Looking up at her, his smile was reminiscent of Harold.

He gestured towards Helen and said, "For example this young lady was ready to end her life only a short month ago. But she learned how to change her thinking and look at her now! She is a successful Senior Councilor for Healing Humanity, Incorporated, specializing in woman's rights."

He paused and then continued, "You know, she takes on a pro-bono case once a month. I believe there's a great likelihood that she will take you on!"

Helen was standing, frozen in her tracks, just watching in amazement and listening as the man spoke.

"Helen, this is Sue," he continued while looking straight at Helen. For a moment they locked eyes. Helen looked into the steel grey eyes and saw a familiar sparkle.

"Yes, angels take many forms," he said to Helen.

Looking back at Sue, he concluded, "Trust me Sue, Helen can help you. You ladies have a nice visit. I have some park cleaning to do."

Helen shook Sue's hand, focused on her for a moment, and then paused to look back at the park maintenance man. He was nowhere to be seen.

She laughed and thought to herself, "I don't know why I bothered to look."

Helen pulled out the handkerchief Harold had given to her and handed it to Sue. "It will be my honor to help you." Helen said, as Sue wiped her face with the angel's handkerchief.

ANGELIC QUILT

A quilt's beauty is in direct relationship to the variety of its colors and shapes united in one piece. So the beauty of community is expressed in different personalities that come together to form a cohesive whole. This is the message from the angels.

We must all learn to celebrate our differences and focus on what we have in common. Any color that stands alone can be beautiful. The colors of a rainbow are made more beautiful by their diversity.

We angels encourage you to join together in true unity. You do this by first creating unity and love in your heart. As you let go of control and allow us, the angels (helpers of the Divine), to assist you, you will more clearly begin to communicate with us. This will bring you to a place of unity in the world.

The message of unity begins with you focusing your energy on your one or two inherent gifts. You cannot effectively do it all. There is only so much energy that you can expend. 100 percent when divided evenly into five areas gives only 20 percent effectiveness in each facet. However, if you focus on the one area in which you feel the strongest pull from Divine Spirit, you will have one hundred percent to give.

Allow yourself for a moment to let go and fly with the angels, seeing the world from our perspective:

You are now high above the landscape, looking down on the scenery below. As you look down, you view the varied tapestry that creates the earth on which you live.

Brown ribbons of silk connect green fields in an intricate patchwork design. Trees dot the landscape giving richness and depth. Tops of houses sparkle and shine in the sun. They appear as jewels sewn in to create an elegant contrast to the earthly design. Newly plowed fields appear as circles of chocolate to break up the pattern of squares and rectangles.

Large bodies of water shimmer as if made of the most exquisite silken threads. As the sun shines down upon them, you feel the pull to dive into their depths, to feel the coolness of the water. Mountains appear in the patchwork design as ripples and lumps creating a unique distinction.

We angels are here to assist you with creating a united community. When you release control, you allow our messages to come through. Then you can weave the strands of your common thoughts through the patchwork of your lives, like a quilter uses several different materials to create a whole.

As leftover pieces off fabric get dropped on the floor and misfit patterns are thrown aside, you must have faith in the Divine plan. We angels will whisper in your ears giving you messages. We will assist at guiding you to pick up these fabrics of your life.

We can help you make them a part of another unique and united patchwork interconnected with others.

This will unveil a community rich in diversity and strong in love. Standing in the power of the messages from the angel, you will find that as you heal others, you have also healed yourself.

ANGELIC ASSISTANCE

In order to get to the other side of life, all must cross the Sea of Uncertainty. Swimming through the Sea of Uncertainty causes many fatalities if you rely solely on yourself. As you swim, your strength begins to leave you and you realize you're not progressing, but only treading water. It feels as if a weight within you threatens to pull you to the depths and drown you. Weariness floods every part of your body and spirit.

Just then, you see someone above you that seems to effortlessly skim across the surface of the Sea. When you cry out for assistance, she calls to you, "Look! There's your angel. Ask her for help!"

A beautiful being of Light seems to hover just above the water. How long she has been there, you wonder. Why couldn't you see her before? As you continue to tread water, barely keeping afloat, you ask the angel, "Will you help me, please?"

Compassion and love are evident in the smiling eyes of this shining being. "I was waiting for you to ask, my dearest one," comes her answer. "When you remember the oneness of all, you become one with your own uncertainties. Only by diving to the depths of your soul and swimming through your own doubts and fears will you be able to release what no longer serves your growth."

Panic rises up in you as you realize you have no strength to deal with the Sea of Uncertainty on your own. Just as a wave washes over you and you begin to go under, the arms and wings of your angel surround you. Peace and power begin to pervade your spirit and body.

With angelic strength inside you, you dive deep. Curiously, the angel energy has enabled you to able to breathe in the blackened depths of the Sea. The angelic light within you shines outwards so you now can clearly see how your fears have functioned as anchors, weighing you down. They have kept you in the depths of despair and agony.

Your angel shows you how to release your fears, one by one. Joy floods through your spirit! In the next moment, you find yourself at the top of the Sea of Uncertainty once more.

Your angel wraps her arms around you; she flies behind you, lifting you higher. You are now able to ride the tops of waves with your Spiritual family, held aloft by your angel. You notice there are many others floating atop the Sea of Uncertainty and that each person that is above the waves is held by an angel. The Sea of Uncertainty is still there, but you travel above it. You know you never have to dive into it again.

You notice other people treading water with desperation on their faces. Hovering above them is a shining angel of Light, eyes full of compassion and love. They seem unaware that their salvation is within their reach, if they could only see and ask for help. Now you understand your purpose. You are one of the many that will help others see and connect with their own angel for their deliverance.

May you see your angel, release your fears and fill your spirit with joy. Then come and join us as we ride the waves of life, skimming over the Seas of Uncertainty, being supported by your angels!

THANKS-GIVING

"Oh, what now?" Mary exclaimed loudly as she went to pick up the phone. The caller ID showed Suzie's name. "Just one evening to myself, that's all I want!"

She took a deep breath, trying to center herself the way she had learned in class the night before. Now it seemed even the stress relief class was creating stress.

As she exhaled, she answered, "Hi, Suzie, how are you?"

"Oh, not so good. I had a bad day at work and a lot of stuff has been going on lately. I just needed someone to talk to," Suzie said sadly.

Mary could sense the tension in Suzie's voice. Every time she talked to Suzie, it was the same subject. The conversation always ended with Mary feeling exhausted! She tried to give Suzie good advice, though she rarely took it.

Bracing herself, Mary asked, "So what's going on?" The next few minutes were filled with the details of the drama in Suzie's life. It seemed that Suzie invited drama and wallowed in it. Mary felt herself growing more and more weary.

Earlier in the evening, Mary had felt energized as she listed on paper all the things she was thankful for in her life. Then she reflected on her blessings, taking slow deep breaths. She actually felt tingles of energy dancing through her body.

At an Angel Empowerment Workshop the night before, Mary learned that if she focused on the things she was grateful for, she would open herself as a divine channel of love. Then, when she gave to another person -- whether it was support, love or even just encouragement – it wasn't her own energy being used, but Divine energy coursing through her body, energizing herself as well as the other person. But all of that was rather distant in Mary's mind as she listened to Suzie ramble on about her troubles.

Mary's head started to pound just as Suzie said, "On top of

everything else, I've had this horrible headache for the past three days!"

Hadn't the workshop leader said that sometimes you can actually take on another's pain if not properly shielded? "I am sorry," Mary managed to say before Suzie continued her monologue.

This gave Mary time to practice what she had learned the night before. She visualized herself in an impregnable pyramid of light where the top reached up to the Divine and the bottom grounded in Mother Earth. She took a deep breath in, visualizing that golden light full of unconditional love entering the top of her head. As the breath flowed down through her body, she could feel her weariness and even her headache dissipating as it exited through the bottom of her feet. She knew the energy was being transmuted into love before going into Mother Earth.

just don't know what I'm going to do," Suzie whined as she seemed to have finished her discourse at last.

This time, Mary she felt energy flow from the top of the pyramid, through her body and into the phone as she answered Suzie. "Suzie, you're the only one that knows the struggles you've gone through and the only one that knows the answers. All I can tell you is that you need to take care of yourself. Why don't you come to the next Angel Empowerment Workshop with me?"

"I'll have to let you know," Suzie said. "I may not have the money."

"Well, be sure to call me and let me know. I need to let you go. I still have to do the dishes. It was good to hear from you," Mary answered.

"Okay, thanks for letting me talk. I actually feel a bit better. Good night," Suzie replied.

Mary was relieved to put the phone down. She took a deep breath and let the tension flow out of her body.

She returned to her list of thankfulness. Why did she have to learn things the hard way, she wondered? As she read each item aloud she began to feel the Divine energy flood her body in a wave of peaceful love.

Mary determined to remain in a spirit of thankfulness. She learned the art of giving with a thankful heart without giving herself away. This way, she could be a pure channel for Divine energy for others, letting the energy from through her instead of from her.

POPSICLE ANGEL

Remember yourself as a small child. Let your mind take you for a moment back to that time in your life. Review the feelings you had as a child. Take a journey with another small child and revisit your emotions as you read the following story.

Sally heard the musical sound of the ice cream truck approaching. As she stood on the porch, she remembered the last time she had asked her mother for money to buy her favorite Popsicle. Her disappointment replayed in her mind as she recalled her mother telling her, "No, not right now, dear."

Sally had watched as the other children ran down the street toward the truck, tears welling up in her eyes and slowly trickling down her cheeks. She had really wanted a Popsicle, but knew her mother would say no, just like the last time.

When Sally's mother walked out onto the porch and saw Sally's tears, she gathered Sally in her arms and asked, "What's wrong, Sally? Aren't you feeling well?"

Sally managed to sob out, "Mommy, I want a Popsicle. But I can't have one, because you wouldn't let me have one last time!"

Sally's mother hugged her tight and said, "Oh, my dear Sally! Last time, you had already eaten too much sugar and had a tummy ache. I didn't want you to feel worse."

"You mean I can have one now?" Sally asked her mother incredulously.

"Of course, my sweetheart. I heard the ice cream truck and was coming out to give you the money. Now you're ready!" came her Mother's reply.

Sally beamed with joy! She took the money and ran to get her treat under the watchful eye of her mother. As she skipped back to the house with her Popsicle, she thought, "Mommy knew I was ready for a Popsicle and she gave me the money for one! I just love her!"

Sally and her mother sat on the porch together as Sally slurped at her Popsicle. She snuggled up next to her mother, looking into her eyes, "Thank you, Mommy. I was afraid to ask you because I was afraid you would say no."

Her mother said, "You know Sally, all you need to do is ask me when you want something. Your job is to ask. It's my job to know if you're ready for it or not. You can always ask, knowing that I will give you only what you're ready for. If I say no, it's because it will hurt you. Then perhaps you will be ready for it later, like today."

Sally said emphatically, "You are the best mommy in the world!"

As they sat, Sally noticed her mother's forehead crinkle. She always did that when she was thinking hard. "What are you thinking about, Mommy? Why are you doing that thing with your forehead again?" Sally questioned.

Her mother laughed and pulled Sally closer. "You never miss a thing, Sally! I was thinking about our Angels. Our job is to ask them for help and they will only give us what we are ready for in our lives," came her mother's reply. "Sometimes they don't give it to us because we aren't ready. But we're always supposed to ask because they love us and want to work with us to bring about the best in our lives," she continued.

"So YOU are MY Angel!" Sally stated emphatically.

"In a way, my dear, just as you are mine," Sally's mother replied with a smile.

LET GO

Becky watched her friends flying high above her head, unburdened by earthly cares. She called out to one of them, "Sue, please help me. I want to fly with you!"

Sue paused in her effortless flight and landed close by. "I can only help you if you're willing to let go," she responded.

Elated, Becky replied, "Yes, yes, I'll let go!"

"Okay, here, take these," Sue said as she handed Becky a beautiful pair of sparkling white angel wings. "The rest is up to you," Sue said with a bright smile as she winged her way to the heavens once more.

Now Becky was overjoyed. At last, she too could fly high and have no worries! Becky carefully fitted the angel wings on her back. As she flexed her back and shoulders, they moved gracefully. Joy flooded her spirit as she felt them grow stronger and stronger with each intake of breath.

Her elation was short-lived though as her beautiful wings beat furiously against the air but barely lifted her from the ground. Why she wasn't she able to lift off as effortlessly as her friend Sue? Becky called out, "I can't get into the air! What am I doing wrong?" The confusion in her face was clearly reflected in her voice.

Sue paused in her flight, hovering for a moment, and called back, "I told you to let go, my dear one.

Becky looked around, wondering what Sue meant. Seeing nothing holding her back, Becky again tried to take flight. Her wings were beating the air so strongly that a few feathers fell to the ground. Looking down at the feathers, she became aware of the chain around her ankle. It had been there as long as she remembered, so she was didn't pay much attention to it. It was locked in place with a huge and heavy padlock. Her thoughts racing, Becky's wondered if the padlock was what Sue wanted her to release. It was locked. How could she possibly let go of the padlock when the padlock wouldn't let go of her?

Now that she was taking a good look at it, Becky's attention was drawn to the other end of the chain. There she noticed were various items that represented her life and thought patterns: her feelings of needing to be in control; her worries about the future and poor self-esteem were all anchored on the chain. Sure, she wanted to change that, but it was padlocked to her leg! Couldn't Sue see there was nothing she could do about it?

She looked up and caught sight of Sue floating and swooping through the air. She called, "Sue, there's nothing I can let go, it's padlocked to my leg! I can't take off."

With that said Becky felt the tears of desperation well up and threaten to flow down her face.

Sue's voice flowed softly on the winds, "It's all in your hands. Just let go! You're holding on too tight and only hurting yourself."

That was all it took for the tears to stream down her face as if a dam had been opened.

"How could Sue be so cruel?" Becky wondered. "Did she give me wings just to tease me?"

The tears continued to pour so Becky reached up with her hand to wipe them away. As she did so, she was aware of a sharp pain in her palm. Wiping the tears caused the pain to intensify. Then she noticed that her hand was tightly clinched around something. She tried to relax and open her hand, but it was closed firmly. Even using her other hand she couldn't open it. With a mounting frustration she held her fist to the sky and cried out, "Help me, please!"

In the next moment, she heard the fluttering of wings and felt a soft kiss on her hand. She looked up into the eyes of the most beautiful angel she had even seen. Tingles of energy surged through her body as peace and relaxation flooded through her.

"The rest is up to you, my love," the melodic voice of the angel sang in her ears. "You have the key, now use it." In the next instant the angel disappeared from her sight.

As Becky brought her arm down, she looked into her now relaxed and open hand.

She gasped as she saw the shiny key in her sore palm. Now she understood about letting go and allowing the peace of the angels to enter her. She had needed the angel's help to relax enough to release her controlling grip on the key. She had always held the key to her freedom.

With trembling hand, she fitted the key into the padlock. A slight turn and soft click released the lock and the chain fell from her ankle with a loud thump. Becky spread her wings again and began to fan the air. As she began to rise higher and higher into the air, tears flooded her face. This time they were tears of grateful joy. She had never felt such lightness in her spirit and body!

Becky flew joyfully to her friend Sue's side. Taking Becky's hands in hers, Sue's exuberant words filled the air. "Welcome, my sister! You have finally claimed your birthright and now fly with the angels!"

ANGEL

WHISPERS

HOW TO GET THE MOST OUT OF THE "ANGEL WHISPERS" PORTION OF THIS BOOK

This is an interactive book with messages channeled through me from Anael. Angels teach in parables and stories. . Many times, Angels speak in simple rhyme. These angel whispers have been given to me over the years throughout some challenging and interesting times in my life. I was instructed to share them here to offer comfort and hope. Flick through the pages. The page that grabs your attention contains your message for the day or week.

The opposite page of the angel whispers is blank. This is for you to record your own personal messages relating to how this angel whisper has helped you that day or week. Be sure to date it and write small because you may have several entries and dates for one angel whisper. I'm sure you will be pleasantly surprised to follow your progress as you sense the angel whispers giving lift to your wings, allowing you to take flight with the angels.

Morgana Starr

ANCIENT MEMORIES

Energies of the Oak run strong and bold
Roots pull up the knowledge of days of old
Telling stories of the Angelic Ones
Of beauties when the world was young

Of dryads, leprechauns, and unicorns,
When the earth was happy and not forlorn
What happened, dear one, why did you walk away
From your magic deep inside and the Angel's way

The rainbow beauty planted deep within
Is waiting to be reawakened and to begin
To bring you out into Angelic Light
Unveiling your potential that burns so bright

When gently do we walk on Mother Earth's soft skin
We will finally understand that we are all kin
Then as we walk the path of the Angelic Ones on high
We will have peace within and whisper a soft sigh
Hand in hand across world upon world
Angels will walk with us with their wings unfurled

NOTES ON YOUR ANGEL WHISPER

Morgana Starr

WORRIES GONE

This day of days has come at last
Today the worries are all past
Now stop and take the time
To see each moment is just fine

You have within your deepest part
All wisdom and a loving heart
In your decision to let Angels guide
You know they will never leave your side

NOTES ON YOUR ANGEL WHISPER

Morgana Starr

ANGEL DAILY MANTRA

All the beauty I have inside
Comes to the surface and cannot hide

Everyone sees the love shining through
In everything I say and do

From this day forth through eternity
Prosperity, health and love will come to me

NOTES ON YOUR ANGEL WHISPER

Morgana Starr

ANGEL HELPERS

Oh the glories I can see
Angels walking beside you and me
Guardian angels assigned as our special guides
All we must do to see is look at our Light inside.

Know now never alone are we ever
From the Angels no one can from us sever.
Just rest in the peace that they give
And walk in their Light and at last truly live.

NOTES ON YOUR ANGEL WHISPER

Morgana Starr

HEALING

Oh that sorrow, deep in your soul!
What has been done to you, no one really knows.
Ripped apart your white washed dreams
Smashed your heart, it does seem.

Many angels it has taken
To help you not feel forsaken
Unfurled wings cover you in soft down
Gives you comfort to know they are around

As they take each piece of your heart
Each one they kiss, so the healing can start.
And gently put it back in place
So their light can show in your face.

Take the time to let yourself heal
Know that Angels your sorrows do feel.
Walk with them and let them comfort you
They will give you peace in all that you do.

NOTES ON YOUR ANGEL WHISPER

Morgana Starr

ANGELS COMFORT

Angels whispering in my ear
Telling me to have no fears
By my side they will always be
Shining their light through eternity.

Negativity no longer rules my life
I am free from all kinds of strife
Prosperity now comes to me
On every level I am free

My angels are my constant guide
They bring success to my side
They help me remember who I am
And gives power to the words "I know I can"

The life I had is a dim haze
Prosperity now fills my days
My thanks I give to angels of light
That has brought me from the night.

NOTES ON YOUR ANGEL WHISPER

Morgana Starr

HEALING ANGELS

See the angels come to me
They wish for an end to my misery.
Encircled now in their pure love
The health they give comes from above.

An Angel reaches her hand to me
Assuring words come so gently
As I continue on my way
She to me does gently say

That my constant friend she will be
I must only open my eyes to see
And ask for help with a grateful heart
The Angels then can do their part

To use their wings and soar with me above
So I am surrounded with the Angel's love
And as the wind whispers in my face
My inner healing I will embrace

I feel the shift within my life
As I let go of my strife
Strength returns and good health is mine
For I know now all things are fine

NOTES ON YOUR ANGEL WHISPER

Morgana Starr

DANCING RAINBOWS

Dancing on Rainbows, up to the stars
Running away till you find who you are
Masters of Light, Masters of Sound
Your own master become, let love abound

Between Heaven and Earth
On Rainbows of Light
Feel the Earth Thump
See the beauty shine bright

Some will listen, some will not
All will leave, with the message caught
On silken webs, like spiders spin
To someday unlock their beauty and light within

Dancing on Rainbows, of Angels delight
Bring out the mysteries, of the inner nights
Dreams long forgotten, now come to the light
So all will learn and know of their forsaken might

Angel's beauty and Angel's light
Do not turn from their love tonight
Know it shines for all to see
None but you is more likely to see

The unfurled beauty and fluttering wings
And to hear the song the Angels sing
Connected together by strands of love
Hearts united by the Angels from above

NOTES ON YOUR ANGEL WHISPER

Morgana Starr

WE ARE ONE

Time moves on and on
You wonder where it has gone
Busy with your own life
No thought to others strife

Think you're independent and strong
Forgetting to all Creation you belong
Pain of the One is the pain of the all
As one gives up so we all do fall

Take a chance, with others share your misery
And also share in all your glorious victories
Though many will never understand
Your spirit must be free from troubled lands

Draw to you all things helpful and good
Rest in the knowing that it is understood
Financial success comes and all will be fine
Also happiness and great health for all time

NOTES ON YOUR ANGEL WHISPER

Morgana Starr

THE MESSENGER

Some days I sit and wonder why
Divine made me, then I will cry
I feel I have no place to go
My path in life I do not know

And then my friend says to me
Without my words she could not see
The Angels whispering on the winds
And Divine life that will never end

Much I see I don't understand
I've been given sight and healing hands
I see right through earth's silken veil
And see the Angels that will never fail

To lift you up in times of need
And help you in all ways succeed.
Now I know what I must do
To spread love the whole world through

I use the gifts given to me
Some I help, though others flee
Bubbling inside trying to break free
Messages with hope to end misery

So as I travel on my road
I share the messages I'm told
The angels sing the songs to me
I, the messenger will simply be

Angel Whispers

NOTES ON YOUR ANGEL WHISPER

Morgana Starr

ANGEL EMPOWERMENT AFFIRMATION

You cannot hold me down
Make me worry or frown
My Spirit must be free
Or I'll die in misery
I let you take me from my goal
And risked losing my very soul
So now I stand strong, firm and tall
With the Angels, I learn to conquer all

I, a victim will no longer be
You have no more hold on me
As I fly on Angel's wings
Divine's Spirit makes me sing

You tried to keep me from my heart's desire
But Angels kept alive my passion's burning fire
Because of you I have become strong
Found strength that was mine all along

No more pain from another will I take
Negativity from you I now forsake
Freedom for me is here now at last
Strife and turmoil a thing of the past

NOTES ON YOUR ANGEL WHISPER

Morgana Starr

ANAEL'S LOVE

Wrap me in your arms so sweet
Let me sit at your dear feet
Anael dearest of the dear
Let me always know you are near

Wrap me safe in your arms of love
With whispers from Angelic Realms above
Take me on flights unknown
Tell me heaven is my home

I hear the sound so pure and sweet
Like the dancing of Angel's feet
And see your star shining bright
Even through the darkest night

Please be my precious guide
With me always do abide
And with Angelic light and sound

NOTES ON YOUR ANGEL WHISPER

Morgana Starr

TRUE TO SELF

When you stifle the song your soul wants to sing
It is like clipping gossamer butterfly wings
You still the beauty of your heart
And from the Angels you stay apart

But to your own self you must be true
Not to do what others say you must do
Walk your path in Angelic peace and love
For your messages come from Angels above

So open your eyes and see the glories all around
As Angels connect you with Divine Light and Sound
At last you can soar through a rainbow filled sky
And finally have the peace you need deep inside

NOTES ON YOUR ANGEL WHISPER

Morgana Starr

UNLOCKING DREAMS

The time has come you know it's true
To find the path that's right for you.
The light you have inside so deep
You no longer to yourself can keep

As through the darkest night you walk
Remember to listen to the Angel's talk
They will hold you firm and steady
Until you know you are finally ready

Dancing rainbows with Angel dust about
Seeing miracles removes all doubt
Unlock the beauty that you are
And know that you never are far

From your dreams becoming reality
Beyond what even you could see
Since you let go of your chains
Never again will life be the same

Anticipation eager in Angelic Heights
Singing to you with all their might
"We are ready...to let Spirit stream
Opening doors to your wonderful dreams"

NOTES ON YOUR ANGEL WHISPER

Morgana Starr

ANGEL'S GIFTS

Thanks to the Angels, I give
For showing me how to live
How to sing in the rain
To have joy amidst the pain

They showed me rainbows in the skies
How to look for fairies sparkling eyes
A world of wonder and delight
To brighten up my darkest night

The gift they gave to me
Was to go inside and see
Divine's true and loving heart
That was mine from the start

Angel Whispers

NOTES ON YOUR ANGEL WHISPER

Morgana Starr

CHOICES

Swimming in a sea of misery
Soon it surfaces for all to see
Consuming your being day after day
'Til you want life to simply go away

You have choices what to do
Whether to create a life anew
Or just stay where you are
And see others joy from afar

Much work it takes day after day
But in misery you don't have to stay
Never alone or dismayed need you be
Because Angels are with you, you see

They give comfort and will be your guide
And will never, ever leave your side
Now as on a healing path you do trod
Each day your step is lighter on this sod

With Angels hand in hand you walk
And with them you can daily talk
And catch a glimpse of what someday you will be
When you are surrounded by Divine's love and majesty

NOTES ON YOUR ANGEL WHISPER

Morgana Starr

SENDING ANGEL'S PEACE

Poor sweet little boy at the busy mall
Pushed around and frightened he may fall
Caught in a world full of turmoil and strife
He looks for comfort from one who brought him life

But caught up in his own misery
The father lashes out for all to see
He curses at the child whose reaching arms
Were seeking only safety from earthly harms

Feeling helpless as I hear the child's bewildered sigh
I call on the power of the Angelic realms on high
To the Divine's precious little soul surround
So he feels peace of the Angels all around

NOTES ON YOUR ANGEL WHISPER

Morgana Starr

DIVINE GIFTS

Angel's magic glistening wings.
Reminds you of the song to sing
Of leprechauns and little elves
Of learning to know your inner selves

Why is it that we want to run away
When Angels want for us joy to play
There is nothing that we have to fear
If we respect them and hold them dear

We have grown up with fear all around
Afraid of shadows and ghosts from the ground
Looking over our shoulders with wild eyes
Noise of our fears blocks the Angel's sighs

They wish for us, our imagination to fly
Allowing access to inherent gifts that never die
To see the faeries, elves, and spirits of trees
Are only a few gifts Divine has given so free

When at last we are in Divine's loving embrace
We wonder why we questioned love and grace
Many things given to us for our help and our joy
We ran from thinking they were part of evil's ploy

So please hear the message clear and bold
To remember the path of the Angel's of old
Forget fear and have joy in every little thing
Then your heart will know the song to sing

NOTES ON YOUR ANGEL WHISPER

Morgana Starr

ANGEL MAGIC

Descended from Fire Goddesses of old
You know of deep mysteries untold
Only take some time to look within
Then your understanding will begin

Out of the darkness you have come
So spread your wings and have some fun
Winging your flight through the cool air
Sprinkling Angel magic from hands so fair

Never forget who you truly are
Honor the road you have taken so far
The joy you have given out so free
Is spread to others, you will see

The music that is deep inside
Is open now and cannot hide
Drifting as wind o'er the plains
To erase all anguish and all pain

NOTES ON YOUR ANGEL WHISPER

Morgana Starr

ANGEL'S WORK

In my heart I hear a song
My life to the Angel's does belong
Their work on earth I freely do
Telling of the messages they have for you.

This morning as I did wake
I felt an Angel my hand take
She tells me, I have much to do
They will guide me the whole day through

Now I feel the energy shift
Since they have given me a gift
The Angels through my eyes do see
Since they have laid their hands on me

NOTES ON YOUR ANGEL WHISPER

Morgana Starr

ANAEL'S LIGHT

What is all this screaming from inside
I was trying to make it hide
I didn't want the world to know
I didn't want my pain to show

But here it comes like a dam has burst
Piling up the garbage and the hurts
Everything around me seems so dark
The world appears forlorn and stark

As I cry out and I lift my hand
I know the Angels understand
Archangel Anael's power she lends
To give me strength, so I will not bend

She calls upon Angelic realms for me
They come to help immediately
And surround me in a shield of love
That connects me to Divine's heart above

I know that she will never from me part
Even in the places of deepest dark
She bring to me Divine's special light
That gives me strength through the long night

NOTES ON YOUR ANGEL WHISPER

Morgana Starr

JUDGEMENTS PAST

Finally the time has come
To bring all peoples into one
To understand that the One they worship and adore
Wants us to live together in peace so we can soar

With the Angels up on high
So to Divine we can draw nigh
Uniting us in our commonality
Living in the Angel's reality

The time for all judgments is past
For we know it is Love that will last
Soar to new heights of understanding and love
Knowing we all are united as One up above

Angel Whispers

NOTES ON YOUR ANGEL WHISPER

Morgana Starr

ANGEL'S ROAD

The road I have traveled has seemed so long
But through my loneliness I have heard a song
That has given me strength through deep dark nights
And shown to me the promise of a Divine light

The song that within my heart does sing
Is the joy that the Angels to me bring
Though turmoil may be all around
The Angel's peace within I have found

My wish is for all others to share
What I have found that lifts my cares
So as I walk upon my path of love
I simply share Angelic messages from above

NOTES ON YOUR ANGEL WHISPER

Morgana Starr

ANGEL POWER

Tears flow down your face like drops of red blood
Waves of sorrow wash over you like a flood
As you march upon the path we call life
You wonder when will be the end to all strife

The answers come when to Angels you do go
Power and strength Angels will to you show
Standing firm as you connect with the Divine
Knowing at last all things with you will be fine

NOTES ON YOUR ANGEL WHISPER

Morgana Starr

BETWEEN HEAVEN AND EARTH

Because of whom you are inside your heart
From Angelic help you will never be apart
And because who you will be tomorrow
Strength you are given to ease another's sorrow

As you work and as you grow
Your path you will finally know
You will remember who you are
And follow the light that shines like a star

Between heaven and earth, in the gap you stand
To bring love, peace and healing to this land
This will help to heal yourself and help heal us all
Because you are willing to say yes to the Angel's call.

NOTES ON YOUR ANGEL WHISPER

Morgana Starr

DIRECTION IN LIFE PATH

Bring out passion from your inner self
Do not let it linger on the shelf
When you learn what you have to give
You will reawaken a reason to live

Angels come to you, these hard days
Strength to help you see through the haze
Angels loving whispers through the night
Will keep you in Divine healing light

Follow their lead as you follow your heart
From their Angelic love you can never part
Unveiled before you, your path you will see
You will know what to and who you will be

NOTES ON YOUR ANGEL WHISPER

Morgana Starr

ANAEL'S PROTECTION

As I cry out and I lift my hand
I know the Angels understand
Anael's inner power and might she lends
To give me strength, so I will not bend.

She calls upon Angelic realms for me
They come to help immediately
And surround me in a shield of love
That connects me to Divine's heart above.

I know that they will never from me part
Even in the places of deepest dark
They bring to me the Angel's special light
That gives me strength through the long night.

Angel Whispers

NOTES ON YOUR ANGEL WHISPER

Morgana Starr

DIRECTION

My dear precious, Angel eyes
You forgot what is inside
Everything you will ever need
For strength in the life you lead

Guardian Angels strong and bold
Give you knowledge from the Ancients of old
Archangels at a moment's notice will appear
To clear obstacles and make your path clear.

Just call upon the strength given from above
They come if you ask and you will feel the love
That is around you each and every single day
That the Divine One sends to light your way

NOTES ON YOUR ANGEL WHISPER

Morgana Starr

COMFORT

Child of sorrow, child of woe
Wondering which way to go
So afraid the choice won't be right
Wanting to make a future that's bright

Dear one, you have forgotten who you are
That your future shines bright as a star
Because your heart is pure and true
Only the best will happen to you

The Angels take your hands in theirs
So you can relieve others pains and cares
Listen to their soft whispers in your ear
Know they love you and have no fears

As you walk with the Angels each day
They send you blessings in many a way
Surrounding you like a cloud, is their love
That is sent from the Divine One above.

NOTES ON YOUR ANGEL WHISPER

Morgana Starr

DIVINE LOVE

Angels Whispering in my ears
Telling me to leave my fears
Far behind and close that door
So I'll be free forever more

When so busy I do get
Then it seems I tend to let
All the worries get in the way
Keeping from pleasures of the day

When I stop and take time to simply be
I know within is my connection to Divinity
Angels are my constant guides and friends
Giving Love and Support until the end

NOTES ON YOUR ANGEL WHISPER

Morgana Starr

LOST CHILD

One day out on the street
A little girl I happened to meet
"Where's my mommy," comes the cry
And then I heard the Angels sigh

She is busy on the telephone
And left her child all alone
To wander out in the streets
And go with anyone she meets.

Children are precious gifts of love
Sent to us from Divine above
They teach us how to live so free
From all earths pain and misery

As the child falls upon the ground
I see the Angels all around
I pick her up and hold her tight
And give her hand a kiss of Light

As I pound upon the door
I watch the child I do this for
Her guardian Angels overtime do work
Cause her mother's duty she does shirk.

As to her mother's arms she does go
I ask Divine protection she will know
And even when she is deep in sleep
Angel's love always will she keep.

NOTES ON YOUR ANGEL WHISPER

Morgana Starr

ALL ARE ONE

We are all sparkles of the Divine Light
Be your path red, green, purple or white
We all blend together to give variety
Many are awakening and will soon see

Angels Flurry...Angels Flight
Wings aflutter with delight
Joy and happiness all around
Hearts opened, love abounds.

NOTES ON YOUR ANGEL WHISPER

Morgana Starr

RAINBOWS

Sunshine and Joy you bring
You make others hearts to sing
As I search the sunbeams all around
I see where the rainbows are found

You make them each and every day
As you send love on its way
For each person that you see
You set a glorious rainbow free

Free to connect all hearts as one
And bask in the healing that's begun
So one day all will live in peace
And inner conflicts will finally cease

Keep that magic deep inside
Angels' joy with you abides
The rainbows beauty all around
Connects us with Divine light and sound

Angel Whispers

NOTES ON YOUR ANGEL WHISPER

Morgana Starr

PROTECTIVE SLEEP

Calling on all Archangels true
All their hosts and guardians for you
While you rest and while you sleep
Protection is there, so safe you keep

Negativity that holds you tight
Will now be led with love to the light
As with fear they struggle not to go
An Angel gently the way does show

Angel's whispering in your ear
Telling you to have no fears
By your side they will always be
And shine their light through eternity.

NOTES ON YOUR ANGEL WHISPER

Morgana Starr

ANGEL RAINBOWS

As you reach for the stars
Don't forget who you are
Surrounded by Rainbows of love
Sent from Angels up above

Follow you where you may
Paths you choose each day
But if life seems to dim
Remember to go within

Find the Angel's power
You're never alone at any hour
Always in a shield of love
Connected to Angels above

NOTES ON YOUR ANGEL WHISPER

Morgana Starr

HEAVENLY EYES

The magic in a baby's eyes
Comes from Divinity's side
For only a short time ago
All things they did know

And in heaven they did live
Existing in the joy they now give
Playing with Angels wings
Hearing Angelic voices sing

So when impatient you do get
Remember why a child does fret
Because he misses that close love
That comes from the Divine up above

Now you know that is a hard act to follow
Showing unconditional love to your little fellow
Love that is pure and soft and sweet
Love you receive at the Divine's feet

NOTES ON YOUR ANGEL WHISPER

Morgana Starr

SOAR WITH ANGELS

As high above the mountains you do fly
Soaring on Angel wings that never die
You have remembered who you are to be
And took a leap of faith for all to see

Though your past is so full of pain
Its ragged memory has helped you gain
The heights upon which you now soar
You recalled what your inner power was for.

Others still choose upon the ground to walk
And the fear within them makes them balk.
On the same level with them you will never again be
Though you encourage them most compassionately
To try their wings and soar with you above
And let them be surrounded with the Angel's love
And as the wind whispers in their face
Their inner healing some will embrace

Alas, many choose accept their fear
Many of whom you hold so very dear
But you must continue in your flight
Spreading love through the dark night

And as you go upon your way
Many will join, and fewer will stay
But you will know in your deepest heart
That you and the Angels have done your part

NOTES ON YOUR ANGEL WHISPER

Morgana Starr

UNHEALED HEALER

Anger bubbles up inside of me
Soon on the surface for all to see
I hold the tears deep inside
For I still want to hide

All the anger and the pain
I went through for another's gain
As the Angels take it on the wind
I know for sure my turmoil will end

Someday I will again give
My life so others can live
But now I will rest and deal
With my inner issues until I heal.

The Angels are singing all around
Bringing me Divine light and sound
And with the Angel's own voice dear
They heal me with their presence near

NOTES ON YOUR ANGEL WHISPER

Morgana Starr

ANGEL LOVE

Angel's breath and wings of love
Created for you from up above
Your heart is sprinkled with Angel's light
As you help others through dark nights

Angel's whispering in your ear
Telling you to have no fears
By your side they will always be
And shine their light through eternity.

NOTES ON YOUR ANGEL WHISPER

Morgana Starr

FAMILY HELP

All this turmoil inside of me
Is plain for others to clearly see
I must take the time to go within
To see the Angels plan begin

They give me peace within the storm
The words I need, they help me form
To bring out the truth for all to see
So the best is done for my family

Angel Whispers

NOTES ON YOUR ANGEL WHISPER

Morgana Starr

WHAT IT IS TO FLY

As I sink into the ground
I now at last all mysteries have found
Why did I have to wait?
Until life was gone and death was my fate?

The beauty on the other side
Was in front of me and did not hide
I needed but to let all judgments fall
And heed the Master's and Angel's call

And someday I will truly know what it is to fly.

NOTES ON YOUR ANGEL WHISPER

Morgana Starr

PROMISES

Worries you have and must let go,
So you will understand and finally know
The peace that comes from within
So the true joy can finally begin.

Wonderful things wait for you and me,
As doors are open for all to see,
The Angels love that is all around,
And the beauty of Divine Light and Sound

Now I can sing
Of angel's magic wings
There is beauty all around
It is waiting to be found

If you look with angel's eyes
You see what none can deny
Who you are and your heart of love
What angels see from up above

NOTES ON YOUR ANGEL WHISPER

Morgana Starr

WORRIES GONE

This day of days has come at last
Today the worries are all past
Now stop and take the time
To see each moment is just fine

You have within your deepest part
All wisdom and a loving heart
In your decision to let Angels guide
You know they will never leave your side

NOTES ON YOUR ANGEL WHISPER

Morgana Starr

FREEDOM

We forgot where our freedom does lie
With the Divine and the Angels on high
When we're wrapped safe in loving arms
We know we are at last free from all harms

Softly, softly Angels whisper to me
Divine's love and acceptance is so free
The love given with no attached strings
Will help you remember your songs to sing.

NOTES ON YOUR ANGEL WHISPER

Morgana Starr

SPIRITUAL GIFTS

Break the chains that hold you down
So you will smile and no longer frown.
With the angels, fly to the sky
Fly up so high, so very high

Way beyond the realms known
To heights none has before flown
The gift of sight and voices you hear
You can speak to others without fear.

Now you sing of what you clearly see
The Angel's song for you and me.
No one can now put you down
Because of the Angels all around.

In the Divine's hands you do reside
Lifted by Angels to Divinity's side
All around you is Divine love
Sent from Divine's own heart above.

NOTES ON YOUR ANGEL WHISPER

Morgana Starr

WISDOM

Wisdom coming from the Sages
Trickles down through the ages
All that you must do is ask
That which you need for each task.

Their wings of softest gentle down
Give peace when you want to frown
They wipe away your falling tears,
And take away your inner fears

Angels walk by your side
Forever they will be your guide
Angels, protection and love to give
So that you will more fully live.

NOTES ON YOUR ANGEL WHISPER

Morgana Starr

CONFUSION

Why do you cry those tears of sorrow?
Lessons are learnt to better your tomorrow
As you learn your own true Divinity
Joy will come, just wait and see.

The Angels around dance with delight
They're your companions through the dark nights.
Ask for their help, they are waiting for you,
To give you peace and hope in all that you do.

Confusion around you like a cloud
Voices screaming, oh so loud.
Some say to walk their way,
Others give you words to say.

Who is wrong and who is right?
Who will help to brighten the night?
Hush, my child, and look within
Your Angels will help to begin.

Guardians you have that are aloft
Angel words come in whispers soft
When in meditation you take the time
Answers you will know and all will be fine

Angel Whispers

NOTES ON YOUR ANGEL WHISPER

Morgana Starr

ANGEL'S FRIEND

Sprinkling sparkles of joy as you walk along your way
Angels sing and rejoice as they watch over you each day
You don't know of your deep inner beauty
And that watching after you, is your Angel's serious duty

Wrapping you in the softest wings of down
They send love to erase your sad frowns.
Rest now dear one, and let others minister to you.
Just hold your Angel's hand and walk your path that's true.

NOTES ON YOUR ANGEL WHISPER

Morgana Starr

INNER LIGHT

Why are all the Angels there?
Sprinkling Angel dust in your hair.
They carefully pick the ones they grace
And bring their beauty to your face.

As you remember who you are
You know they brought you safe this far
The Angels all around you sing
As miracles to you they bring

That which you seek to hide
The part you cannot abide
Bring it now into the open Light
Though it is from the darkest night

Hidden you can now no longer be
You must show yourself for all to see
In the mirror you smile so bright
As you glow with Angelic Light

NOTES ON YOUR ANGEL WHISPER

Morgana Starr

AFFIRMATION

Negativity no longer rules my life
I am free from all kinds of strife
Prosperity now comes to me
On every level I am free

The angels are my constant guide
Bringing success to my side
And help me remember who I am
Giving power to the words "I know I can"

The life I had is a dim haze
Prosperity now fills my days
My thanks I give to the Angels of light
That transformed my life from the night.

NOTES ON YOUR ANGEL WHISPER

Morgana Starr

ANGEL EYES

Swimming in a sea of misery
Soon it surfaces for all to see
You have choices what to do
Whether to create a life anew

Or just stay where you are
And see others joy from afar
Much work it takes day after day
Though in misery you don't have to stay

But never dismayed need you be
Because Angels are with you, you see
They give comfort and will be your guide
And will never, ever leave your side

Now as on a healing path you do trod
Each day your step is lighter on this sod
With the Angels hand in hand you walk
And with them you do daily talk

From the Angels' eyes a glimpse you see
Of what someday you will finally be
When you shine with Divine inner Light
Surrounded by Angelic protection and might.

NOTES ON YOUR ANGEL WHISPER

Morgana Starr

HEALING TOTEM

Healing now is to begin
Stop the pain from coming in
All around is love and light
That takes you through the darkest night

Can you hear the warrior angel's cry?
The sound makes brave men want to fly.
It is the coming of your power
That you can call forth in this hour.

NOTES ON YOUR ANGEL WHISPER

Morgana Starr

PROSPERITY

My angels pull me out of every mess
And their love for me to all confess.
They comfort me with gentle touch
And tell me why I matter so much

On this bright and starry night
I ask for the blessings of angels light
To break the veil of negativity
And to bring to me prosperity

I just rest in their downy soft wings
And listen as they softly to me sing
Of how prosperity and healing love
Was brought to me by the angels above

NOTES ON YOUR ANGEL WHISPER

Morgana Starr

I FORGOT

Trickling down the cheek they come
A trail of tears that block the sun
There is sorrow deep inside
That I can no longer hide.

It feels like layers being pulled from me
And now it is open for all to see.
Vulnerable, deep runs the pain
Fear that others will use it for their gain.

When will I see the healing begin?
Or do I just want my life to end?
Who will I call on in my hour of need?
Where will I get help in work and deed?

I forgot about the Angels on who I may call
They lift me up; when on my face I fall
I must rest in their downy soft wings
And listen as they softly to me sing

NOTES ON YOUR ANGEL WHISPER

Morgana Starr

ANGEL PROTECTION

Angel's are watching over you
Helping you find the path that's true
To keep your feet on solid ground
And feel the peace that is all around

Walk in the freedom of unconditional love
With the angels whispering from above
That you now can never ever fall
For Angels hold you when you call

Angels whispering in your ear
Telling you to have no fears
By your side they will always be
And shine their light through eternity.

NOTES ON YOUR ANGEL WHISPER

Morgana Starr

STRENGTH

Softly, softly Angels whisper to me
Divine's love and acceptance is so free
The love given with no attached strings
Will help you remember your song to sing.

Angels send to you for these hard days
Strength that will help you see through the haze.
And their whispers of love through the night
That will help keep you in Divine healing light.

Precious One, Angels lift you high
Higher than even eagles can fly
High up to the Divine One's arms
Where you will always be safe from harm

Angel Whispers

NOTES ON YOUR ANGEL WHISPER

Morgana Starr

TRUE LOVE

Love elusive as the wind
Romantic tales that never end
Seeking true love to receive from another
To have a love deeper than any other

Unconditional love is all around
Stop and listen to the sound
Of Divine's and Angel's unconditional love
That comes as softly as the whisper of a dove

And as loudly as the thunder in the storm
Although we want for it to take human form
We hold inside of us what we seek
All we must do is take a peek

Then within ourselves we are whole
Not needing completion from another soul
Then you are ready for a partner in your life
One that is healed and free of strife

NOTES ON YOUR ANGEL WHISPER

Morgana Starr

HEART TO HEART

Sometimes I just sit and wait
Wondering what will be my fate
Knowing that the power's mine
To take control, then I'll be fine.

Divine has given me my gifts
And I can use them as I see fit
So now I sit with thankful heart
Knowing from Divine I'll never part

Peace flows in Angel's whispering winds
Now at last all inner turmoil will end
Then comes Divine's overwhelming love
Sent to me through the Angels above

Sweeping all the fear away
Knowing comfort I'll feel each day
When again I sit in misery
I know Angels I will surely see

NOTES ON YOUR ANGEL WHISPER

Morgana Starr

ANGEL WHISPERS

Angels whispering in my ear
Telling me to have no fears
By my side they will always be
And shine their light through eternity.

Waves of love flood me completely
Compassion fills the Angel's eyes for me
For what we have to see us through
Is already inside of me and you

Comfort given, you can receive
If you only will just believe
In Divine unconditional love
That comes straight from above

NOTES ON YOUR ANGEL WHISPER

Morgana Starr

DIVINE EXPRESSION

Divine's own heart is our heart too
So very close to me and you
Love Divine sent from the ground
To see this you must look around

At the trees and little plants
Bugs, insects, and the ants
What you see around you every day
Are expressions of Divinity here to stay

NOTES ON YOUR ANGEL WHISPER

Morgana Starr

LOVE

Love and Light
Comes to you on this Darkest Night
Know the Angels up above
Wish you nothing but their dear love

See them shimmer in the air
As they lift all your cares
No more to live in dark misery
Angels will help you be free

Angels love is all around
Fear and guilt can't hold you down
Divine's love so full and free
Manifests itself to you and me

Unconditional Love is meant for you
Divine's gift to walk your path that's true.
With Angel's help you have inner peace
So struggles within can at last cease.

NOTES ON YOUR ANGEL WHISPER

Morgana Starr

ASSISTANCE

Sparkling laughter Angels bring to my door
Heavenly beauty and so much more.
Looking around I can now see
What was always in front of me

Protection from the angels up above
Surrounded by Divine's own dear love
When I get caught up in mundane days
I forget to look through my created haze

To see what Divine has put there for me
Unconditional love, protection and gracious beauty
So now I take the time for thanks to give
For Angels who remind me of the life I can live

Never to let the mundane rule
Remembering to use spiritual tools
With help from the angels day by day
And letting Divine wisdom light my way.

Angel Whispers

NOTES ON YOUR ANGEL WHISPER

ANGELIC ENCOUNTERS

Angels make themselves available to help us throughout many circumstances in our lives. They appear to us as a kind stranger, a doctor, a voice, or even a dragon. They come in a form that we need at the time. Sometime they simply leave behind mysterious unexplainable little messages to lift our spirits.

Some may choose to call these experiences a coincidence. Some may think it is the working of an overactive imagination. I choose to believe it is the beauty of an angel exhibiting love and compassion on our life's journey

The following are some inspiring stories where people have experienced the extra ordinary touch of an angel bringing peace to their hearts.

ANGELS WALK AMONG US

In February of 1965, a visit to the doctor's office revealed lumps/cysts in my breast. This definitely wasn't something a 25 year-old mother of two daughters was expecting. Just 24 hours later, I found myself in a private room on the cancer floor of a local hospital, awaiting surgery at 8:00 A.M. the following morning.

A million thoughts went through my mind that long evening. I came to the realization that my life was totally in God's hands and the outcome from the scheduled surgery would determine the path my life would take going forward. If everything came back benign, I would return home and pick up where I left off in my daily activities. But if there was cancer present, I would be venturing into the unknown.

All alone, feeling helpless, I began to pray. I looked upwards, saying, "Thy will be done!" Instantaneously there appeared at the foot of my bed a brilliant golden-white light, as bright as the sun. Its radiance went from floor to ceiling and was the width of the hospital bed. Suddenly a rush of heat entered through the crown of my head, traveled through my entire body, and exited my feet. That experience left behind a feeling of peace and tranquility that has endured for the past 45 years.

I was wheeled into surgery the following morning. When the doctors opened me up, they found nothing. There were no cysts or lumps that had been seen on the x-rays. All they found was an infection in the milk ducts. And I couldn't tell them about my "Visitor" the night before because I'm sure they would have considered transferring me to the psychiatric ward.

I had been blessed by an angel with a miracle healing. Little did I know that I had also been blessed with other spiritual abilities that did not surface until a few weeks later. One of these was receiving information from God, Jesus, Mary, and angels. It was the beginning of a journey in service to my Creator.

In 1979 I was told, "From this day forward my child, you shall work for Me full time writing My words in books." This came to pass with the completion of 21 books, plus articles I've written for other publications. Currently His words are conveyed to people through greeting card messages.

Since my miraculous healing I have traveled many roads to spiritual enlightenment. Along the way I was introduced to working with all of the "gifts of the Holy Spirit." These are being used to help mankind; I am only the vessel through which God works. And yes, there have been times when angels have appeared in many disguises, each arriving unexpectedly, performing a task to be done and then disappearing, never to be seen again.

Never doubt the power of God! He still performs miracles and His angels indeed walk among us! That is the truth!

By Beverly Hale Watson

ANGEL MECHANICS

When I was around 30 years old, I had just had my baby girl. We were broke and didn't have enough money to finish the week out till payday – no gas to get to work or food to eat. I silently prayed, "Please, only 20 dollars would get us through the week."

Our in-laws lived down the street from us, not very far. We were taking the kids there to play with their cousins while the adults played a few hands of cards. We were down and depressed as we pulled up to the gas station to put the last dollar and fifty cents in the tank for gas.

Suddenly, a car pulled up with two tall blonde men in it. I couldn't see them well as they got out and went to talk to my husband, Russell. Russ had the car hood up and was checking on something in the engine.

They asked for a jump for their battery. He thought that was weird since they had just driven up, but he jumped their car anyway. They talked under the hood again, and then they drove away.

Russ looked flabbergasted as he climbed back in our car. He handed me a 20-dollar bill. He said that he refused the money at first and had told them he would've helped anyone. However, they insisted that he take it. I know they were two angels!

By Donna Hunter

DAD'S ANGEL

It was October 2009, when we received my father's diagnosis of terminal cancer. The doctor gave him four to six months to live. I moved in. It was the time to be caregiver to a man who took care of his family most of his life. He fought in the Korean War and survived, but this cancer was going to kill him.

My father was a tall, robust man who was strong in his convictions. He was a hard worker; most of the time working six to seven days a week just to take care of his family. I don't think that he believed in the Divine until his illness.

As my father's illness progressed I noticed him going further within. He was separating from us and preparing to go the next realm. I would notice him conversing while lying in bed with someone. Who was he talking to? He would raise his arms in the air like a conductor telling me how beautiful the music was. I believe he was talking with the Angels and they were leading him home.

One day he was sitting at the table with my mom and he leaned over to give her a kiss. I took a picture because it was such a poignant moment so full of love. I knew the end was near and I wanted to capture the moment.

When the picture was placed onto the computer we saw all around my father this radiant white light. The kitchen in my parent's house was dark; no lights were on, so this glow around my father had to be his angel. It was the most beautiful picture I have ever seen. Dad died peacefully thanks to his angels who were with him. I am forever grateful to the angelic realm.

By Cynthia Abruzzo DeSiena

HOSPITAL ANGEL

I had an out of body experience when I was 11 yrs old. I went through some major surgery. I was born with a twisted ribcage and the doctors had to take out cartilage and reshape my ribs. When I went under the knife (so to speak), I saw lights. They looked like Christmas lights twinkling. Then I blacked out.

Then I saw a black figure looking down at me. A peaceful light surrounded this being as it shone down on me. I couldn't see the face or the color of the hair as it was blacked out. But I knew he was male and he had long flowing hair, blowing in the wind.

I tried talking to him but I couldn't speak. Nothing came out of my mouth. Then I woke up in the hospital room in recovery. Someone told me that I almost died but I survived. On the counter next to me was a teddy bear that I have to this day. Nobody knew where the teddy bear came from.

Then it hit me. Oh my god... I was saved by an angel!

By Katherine Kovacs

SURGEON'S ANGEL

My name is Andrea de Michaelis and I publish Horizons Magazine which is Florida's mind/body/spirit magazine since 1992. I'm also a professional psychic medium, and my jobs are relevant to my story since I am long years in the genre of the mystical and the paranormal. I know that angels and ghosts exist and I also know that not every story that every person tells is true. That makes me a skeptic, as well.

I don't tell angel stories. I don't tell every time I receive unseen assistance or reassurance. I tell those only when I use them to illustrate a point. I know so many attention-seeking people, always telling grandiose stories of their paranormal adventures. I'm only interested in a story if it was something that made you rethink a segment of your life and make a change because of it. So here's the first angel story I've ever put to paper.

In 2004, I was in the hospital over the Christmas holiday waiting to get my gall bladder out. I had a specific zero fat diet I was allowed, with no deviation or they could not do the surgery. So on Christmas Eve and Christmas Day, they scheduled and delivered the wrong meals to me, which I knew I couldn't eat. Since a lot of the regulars had the holiday off, I could not find anyone with authority to get into the kitchen to bring me anything other than one serving of Jell-O. Finally, on Christmas Day, being the sixth day I hadn't eaten anything other than clear broth and the one Jell-O the day before, I called a friend to please bring me two bananas.

Even though they were not doing what should have been done and my surgery was being jeopardized because of what they were doing, I didn't blame anyone for what was happening to me. I had a different mindset about it. The predominant thought that kept crossing my mind was that although it appeared that no one cared about me right then, God had it all under control. I'd been on morphine the entire week before, so my spidey sense was non-existent. But I figured it was a test and if I held faith and thought of a favorable outcome, I'd be fine getting through whatever I had to get through.

When morning came, I was wheeled into the prep room and I was relaxed from the valium they've given me. It was a pleasantly bright white room and my glasses were off, so the scene was a little fuzzy and soft focus. I think it's also the recovery room, as there are maybe a dozen other patients in beds at the other end of the room. Some of the nurses seemed quite tall and moved in the same motions.

My surgeon, Dr. Patrick Domkowski from Omni Medical Care in Palm Bay, walked over to say hello and I saw that the very tall figure behind him was not a nurse but an angel! She was maybe seven and a half feet tall and twice as wide as the surgeon. So as he stood talking to me, the angel was behind him. He was almost in silhouette because of her brightness, but he was bright, too. Not a blinding white light, just a glow from inside, but definitely enough to be noticed.

I could see that the angel was attached to him. The ones I saw earlier didn't seem attached. As soon as I think, "she's attached to Dr. D.," she shows me the thought that he's Catholic and he prays before surgery. I figured she was my sign that my faith was not in vain, since I held it when there was no evidence to support it. I held my faith even though there was evidence that things were not going my way. My surgery went fine, and as a result of it I changed my entire lifestyle and eating habits. I've never been healthier or happier.

When I saw Dr. D the next day, the angel was still with him. She smiled as though we had a secret. He asked how I was doing and I told him I knew he was Catholic and prayed before surgery and I thanked him. When I went for my follow-up visit at his office two weeks later, I told him what I'd seen and how I knew. I told him I didn't want to discuss it; I just wanted him to know. I got the sense he knows he's covered.

By Andrea de Michaelis

ANGEL DOODLING MESSAGE

My name is Marita and this is what happened to me when I was a college student, over 30 years ago.

It was about 1975 and I was living in Woodburn, OR. I was going to college in Salem. It was a Saturday morning about 10 or 11, and I was getting ready to drive home to see my Mom and Dad. I just felt so happy that day and so ready to just live. I was singing and praying, telling God that I just saw Him as Creator of all and everything was perfect. I was just feeling so grateful.

I got out of the shower, wrapped myself in a towel, went in my bedroom and opened the shade. There in the fog on the window was a stick figure with a smiling face and dancing legs and arms extended and bent. There were three exclamation marks at an angle next to it. It was on the inside of the window and the figure was drawn in the fog. It looked like it had been drawn with a pinkie finger. The lines were quite thin but very distinct and it was about 10 inches high and 4 inches wide.

I had opened that same shade everyday for months before and never had this been there in the fog. I lived there for another year and it never again happened because after that I checked each morning just to make sure.

I called my mom to tell her I was sure an angel had done this. Of course, she tried to reason me out of believing it had been an angel visitation by saying "No, maybe the shade left a mark that looked like it." or "Someone had left it years before and the fog just made it reappear." But that couldn't have been it because I tested those theories out for weeks afterward and never again was it there.

I still can picture it perfectly in my mind, exactly what it looked like. It was for sure tied to the praying and feeling of complete trust and gratitude that I had that morning. It just felt so perfectly peaceful and right that day.

I lived on the second story of that house in Woodburn and there were no roofs to climb on outside to reach the windows or any other way to get in my house. It had automatic deadbolts. Every time the door was closed, they were secure. There was a separate locked entrance at the bottom of the staircase and another locked door at the top.

So I know it was not a person who wrote in the fog that day, but had to have been an angel, just reminding me all was well and my prayers were heard. That is all I can think of that it could have meant. To this day I still feel that it was my guardian angel.

By Marita VanSmoorenburg Shaffer

GUARDIAN LAUNDRY ANGEL

This happened to me about 25 years ago. My three children were small, about three, five and eight years old. I was a busy stay at home mom and had a childcare business in my home for six other children. We always had lots of fun going on field trips and going swimming at the public pools.

That evening after a busy day, I had lots of laundry to do. I had an older washer and it bounced around a lot when it was in the spin cycle and would often get off balance. It made a loud beeping sound when all the laundry bunched up on one side so I was always nearby while running a load. We had just run a new gas line from the water heater to a used dryer, a gift from a friend when the old electric dryer broke. I was thankful I could dry our clothes at home again instead of making a trip to the laundry mat.

My ex-husband would get angry if things were not done properly so I was usually careful about doing the laundry properly and putting it away promptly. That particular night I had lots to do and wasn't thinking about order. I put in a load to wash before bedtime and didn't check it or stay up to wait for it to dry. I decided I would dry it in the morning because I was so tired.

That night I had a lot of trouble sleeping. In my dream, someone was telling me to wake up and shaking me. I could actually feel the shaking and hear the voice. I thought one of the children needed me and my husband wanted me to check on them. So I rolled over and asked him, "Are you calling me?" But I continued to hear the voice and the shaking became urgent.

I realized he was sleeping soundly and then I was awake enough to smell something like rotten eggs. I then woke him up and asked, "What is that horrible smell?" He was instantly awake and said "Its gas! Get the kids outside now and don't turn on any lights!"

He ran around the house opening windows and checking for a leak while I was outside with the children. He found that the washer had jumped over towards the dryer and slightly knocked open the lever to the gas line. The house had filled with gas!

We stayed outside for a long time, even though it was about five in the morning. I told him about the dream and how I knew it must have been my guardian angel waking me up. I was so thankful for that dream and my angel calling and shaking me. Needless to say, I never did laundry without checking it every few minutes after that!

By Marita VanSmoorenburg Shaffer

SHIELDING WITH ANGEL LOVE

One day I was working with a client, and what came upon me was an energy that took over my body to the point that I felt detached. My mind was fading into a deep dark abyss, somewhere in a distance that could not be measured. The only way to describe it in the most simplest of definitions would be Possession.

I immediately called upon my guides to help me through this ordeal, and received no response. Then calling upon Archangel Michael, I heard a voice say, "Yes, Misty, I can cast this away, but I won't. This is your path, and you must learn how to deal with such matters."

I was told that I was dealing with the energies of this person's demon. This was a manifestation of fears that had now created an entity that was attached to her very being.

Archangel Michael said to me, "I will instruct you in what to do, but I will not do it for you."

I was told to swallow the demon, to allow it to walk through my light, and transmute its frequency to a higher vibration. This was sending bells off in my head, making me apprehensive to do so.

But then Archangel Michael said to me, "We must love the demon as well, for they need love, too. The only protection we ever need is the love of ourselves which is our true light within. That will always cast away any darkness looming."

Of course this frightened me, but I did exactly what was instructed, taking my light from within and shining it forth. Within seconds I felt myself become more aware of my body, and the internal screaming I had initially felt, left me like water draining from a tub.

It was one of the most profound experiences for me, and taught me love in the most unconditional way of love to be found.

Michael said to me, "Misty, most of you protect yourselves,

shielding yourselves and your hearts. Your heart and your love without the judgment of what is wrong or right, or darkness and light, are the greatest attributes of your spirit, and the pure connection of God. To love no matter what, is to love yourself, and everything else. Love when it hurts. Love when you feel weak. Love the vulnerability of your being, and see how you are released, and empowered by God."

By Misty Dawn

ANGEL DRAGONS

It was some years ago when my husband and I moved to another state from Florida and I met with a few ladies who were starting a Master Mind group. We five decided to pursue Master Mind as an avenue for healing our past and producing a better future. So began seven years of weekly meetings. We became close trusted friends who grew individually and together and became more confident in the world and in relationships because of our work and safe processing through the Master Mind method.

My husband and I moved back to Florida ten years ago and I have kept up a close email relationship with one member in particular, you guessed it, Kathryn. She had had a particular difficult childhood, none of which need be mentioned here. Suffice it to say it left her timid, disempowered, and victimized emotionally, even in her later years.

As the support group that we all were to each other, she came more and more out of her shell and was able to stand up for herself in her current situations. She saw all of us as powerful women who did not take abuse even though we had also been victims as children. When our own "herstories" became known to her, she saw that if we came out of it empowered, she could too.

I know her today through our email connection and find that she now is able to be an at-home healer and indeed, works diligently on her family members energetically and any and all who show up for her needing healing energy. She herself does better without extensive connections with people and continues to work on her emotional issues with such true courage and bravado that sometimes I am still surprised by her gutsy ability to keep going in spite of whatever shows up. Yes, better because of Master Mind however at the current time she prefers to keep to herself at home as that has become her safety net. This is how she finds herself as self-empowered.

It is important to understand that it is not necessary to push one's self out in the world to show off empowerment if the core self experiences that from the inside. She has found her place in the physical world that is a comfort for her.

Recently she got a summons to serve jury duty. She wrote to me in a panic, not wanting to go but feeling the old authority mandate pushing down on her with heavy obligation. I wrote back explaining ways to avoid jury duty if she so chose but left her to make her decision, as it should be.

Now to back track a bit here, from our 10 years of emails (plus our Master Mind years together) we had really gotten to know each other. We had spoken about Resourcing Ourselves, which is finding situations, books, experiences, and people, whatever that we could use as a support mechanism during difficult times. That could mean something as simple as a trip to the spa or a candlelit hot bath, talking with a friend, using EFT, meditation...well, you get the idea. We all were experts at finding Resources.

As one of my supports to her, I had sent her a dragon greeting card (blank inside) of a beauteous purple dragon in flight. She immediately knew to personify the dragon as her Resource and the dragon moved out of the card for Kathryn and became named as 'She'.

Some time had passed from when 'She' had become part of her life. Off and on in emails, she would mention that 'She' had landed on her shoulder during a tense moment and calmed her down. Sometimes Kathryn would share that "She" was able to give words she could not think of during a fretful conversation. (Her in-law family members are very dysfunctional as well) I never even intended or thought she would use that casual support card I had sent as such a powerful help for her. Let alone that through it she would find her angel dragon personified in her life to assist her in any battle she had to contend with.

Once I had gotten a number of emails from her lauding 'She' as such a warrior dragon I found a ceramic figure of a blue dragon, somewhat cute and sweet at the same time, and knew I had to send that to Kathryn. Well, 'Blue Boy' as he so called himself became an additional angelic help for her whenever she needed some support.

So lo and behold, as she wrote to me after all was said and done with the jury duty summons, her triumphant victory in facing courageously, yet again, one of her most difficult challenges. Here is what happened.

Kathryn has not driven for years and uses the public transit system whenever she needs to get anywhere. On that fated day, without squeezing out of jury duty the way I let her know she could, she boarded the bus at 6:30 A.M. and headed to the courthouse WITH 'She' and Blueboy on each shoulder, championing her onward. Word after word was softly whispered into her ears with encouragement that she could do this.

Please understand that authority is Kathryn's biggest challenge. She had always cowered and backed off, drawing a blank mind, to those she believed to be more important than her. Now with the angelic 'She' and Blueboy in the form of dragons to back her up into empowerment, she faced this previously terrifying situation.

You guessed it. The court authority she spoke to when she arrived at the courthouse, told her that she would not be needed that day. This particular jury duty roster had been filled. She could then go home.

Not only did her angel dragons assist her in finding her own courage to face her biggest foe, but on some level allowed the challenge to collapse so that she did not even have to be on the jury panel.

To this day my friend Kathryn is my hero and champion, my best example of "Yes, I can do it" whatever it is. She herself has resourced what she needed to let her life be full and meaningful. As an energy worker myself, I can promise you that 'She' and Blueboy are as real as you and I. They may live in

another dimension but for Kathryn, not so. They live in her world and share her strong square shoulders as their home.
By Susan Solivan

MESSAGES

FROM

ANGELS

An Angel called White Feather

Channeled by
Lisa Johnston-Anderson

THE PATH

You don't have to scream you are the victor to be one, but never accept that your defeat is inevitable. It is not...we will not be defeated, yet no one is the victor. Time will continue on and this will be the path over and over now as it always was.

This is what we do, take and give...receive and lose. It all has its balance. Love and light is to balance darkness and hatred. Not a battle in winning, but a battle in being. We have always been, will continue to be.

Miles matter not as distance is in the heart not the path. Still now see things as not being in the form as your body demands you to see, but in the reality of how your spirit knows it shall always remain.

THIS TOO WILL PASS

My children, heavy is the sadness and despair you now shelter within your hearts. The burden has yet much more weight to place upon you. Fear not this time as desolate as it may seem.

A time before you remember you chose these lessons with all awareness and conviction. It is a choice made with complete confidence of your soul's ability to weather any storm, even storms with fury as the likes that you may face now.

You are children of the gods, learning, growing, ascending back to your rightful places. Be strong and have faith in yourselves, faith in your strengths and faith in your beliefs. Soon the time will come that will leave you standing once again proudly at our side, feeling as if you can conquer all the odds and all your demons at once. There is a simple reason for why you feel the way you do, because my beloveds…you can.

~White Feather~

Shandie's Angel

Channeled by
Shandie Savage

ANGELIC LOVE

I am the wind that whispers over the land, gentle and fierce, passionately serene. I am the song whispered by the night about the glory of the sun. I am the water that caresses and crushes with mystical flowing and ancient knowing.

I am the young body with the very old soul. I am the old body with the dancing playful young spirit. I am the gentle depths hidden silently within and the abrasive shallowness raging without.

Where there is dark I am the light. Where there is light I'm hidden from obvious sight...frolicking somewhere in a not so distant night. Where there is chaos, I am harmony. As I am chaos, so too are the reactions from all that I touch.

As I am peace the world around me sleeps sweetly tucked in dream bliss and stardust blankets. I am the balance and the change. I am familiar to much of the strange.

I am the secret no one can keep but everyone shares. I was the pillow where once you did weep when you thought no one cared. I am the ray of sunshine that pierced through the clouds to bring you peace.

I am your comfort and I am your pain. I am the whispers of your heart that your ears never hear but your spirit always feels.

I am all this is and all that was, and I give birth to all that will be. I am the love inside of you and inside of me.

~Shandie's Angel~

Cynthia's Angel

Channeled by
Cynthia Segal

LOVE YOURSELF AS MUCH AS I LOVE YOU

"Love thy neighbor as thyself" was meant to express the importance of loving yourself, or you will be shown your love for yourself in the reflection of your neighbor/partner/child.

Sometimes, we are afraid to love ourselves unconditionally because our upbringing puts us in conflict with that idea, that feeling.

We began as a self-loving creation. We began as love.

Close your eyes and look inside for your beauty. Release your stories of should be taller, or smaller, or lighter ~ release your stories.

God has already judged you, and found you perfect. We will whisper this message to you forever. Your love of yourself will create your world reflections. It is doing so now.

To change your reflection, change your heart, change your words and change your thoughts. Smile. Relax. Breathe.

We are with you always. We are here for you. Look inside your heart, you will see us there; waiting for you to see us.

We see you, we love you, we will always be with you ~ safely in your heart.

Love yourself as much as we love you.

YOUR DREAMS ARE WHAT BROUGHT YOU HEAR

Your dreams are what brought you here. Can you still hear them, in the quiet moments before you wake? In the still hours of the night? In your heart?

Dream little one, dream on. Dream of what makes your heart happy. Dream of beautiful sights and sounds and feelings, beautiful smells and moments.

Your life is your gift to yourself; your breath a gift from creation ~ because we all believe in you. We are here with you to support you. You have only to ask.

Ask us to demonstrate what a full heart feels like. Ask us to show you what laughing is until you know what sore cheeks feel like. You are asking, all the time. We are answering, all the time.

Reach for a better feeling thought, a happier request, a more joyful demand from your life ~ you deserve it! The best is yours, only allow yourself to receive it.

Love yourself as much as we love you.

~Cynthia's Angel~

Archangel Azrael

Channeled by
Rebecca Snavely

CALL TO RELEASE

This is the time of giving away...The Great Giveaway is not in materials, but in love and surrender of all that binds and weighs spirit. Inner rest can be found and achieved if sought by the eye and arm of contentment. Take no more than is needed, and give more than that. It is the passing through of things that lifts the soul.

Do not hesitate. Do not wait. But show the way through silent grace. The heart will lead. The mind will follow. Spirit will guide for the Torchlight burns. It is an inward purging. And ask not, "Why me?" It is Creator who brought you here from the depths of Creation. You are worthy of all tasks laid before you. Seek the Higher Calling of that which you now face. Beware of distractions. Worldly tasks are not a concern. Align them with intent in Heart. Discard what cannot be aligned.

Make no mistake: Only The Maker restores!

Dance, sing, shine, fly, and flow through life. Notice the words, "trudge, stumble, struggle," do not enter here. Life is not meant to be that. Let the light in you see the light in the world. Connect and be the weave of love...the tapestry. You are where you are to show someone the Divine Truth of their Being, through you...through your grace of being. Paint the song in your heart on you, so the world can see the portrait of your prayer through you. It is the magic you possess; the magic to create wonder. Miracles will abound.

You are called out from your slumber. You will not lose what you cannot bear but will lose what you bear in fear. In fear, there are no buffers. What you fear and struggle to protect yourself from in action, only serves to bind it to your heart by your own hand. Break the fetters within. That is the key to protection. You are not yet who you are. You are more.

Let the voice of your heart rain down on the barren land and a thousand voices will join you. That which one seeks to destroy, will certainly find him. You have forgotten that you are one with Creation and the garden of life can flourish abounding all around you, manifesting in mankind. The seeds lie in everyone. Starve no one of the joy that is in you.

I call you out to achieve the Promise of Old, for you have forgotten it is fulfilled in you, through you. To wait for something to happen, is futile and accomplishes nothing.

CALL TO EXPLORATION

Remember all that you now hold out of fear, is that which surely holds you. All that you see is the illusion. All that you do not yet see is what is. The realness in you, of you, is that which you do not see. Reflections of now guide the way Home to your Heart of Truth and the Essence of your soul. The Remembering is what fuels your fire—the blue flaming inferno within. It is the source of Inner Truth—the Divine Truth of your being.

Live as you truly are not what you fear or believe life has made you. Sing your own Heartsong, not the one given and taught by others. It resonates not with your spirit. It can only bring dis-harmony. The Power of Creation is you.

The time has come. Now go and do wonders. Go and Be Wonders! You want to go, but you have to let go, in order to go. If you yearn to go, but linger and refuse to let go, you are imbalanced on your feet and you will surely fall.

You cannot dive deeper and explore the wonders that await you by holding on to the surface. New discoveries are not brought to the world or self that way. Dive deep like a dolphin and come back to the surface with the knowledge that will guide the lost ships at sea. This is how you heal the world.

Show, like the dolphin, with inspiring leaps and playful joy. They will follow you.

Yours is not the way of struggle. Resume that path no more. Be the dancing light. Follow the torchlight into the caverns of your soul. Seek and find the beauty and secrets that are there. The great crystal structures formed by the water of your tears are strong and inspire. They hold and sustain a bounty of life you do not know. It is a storehouse of secret treasures to behold. This is where you find the streams of pure living water—in the chasms of your soul.

Go through the Gateway, the Portal, to be made whole. Let go, in order to go forward. Go forth with the Heart of Truth. Seek not the ways of old, for they only enslave your being, but seek in the places of old to find the gifts that set you free.

CALL TO ACTION

Find the source of your wounds and heal them through the reflections of Now. Remain grateful for them. It is the pain that draws attention to that which needs healed. It is the anger that draws attention to that which needs healed. The Passage of time backward is not easily traversed. It winds; sometimes spirals but always forms golden threads in the beautiful tapestry of your life. The light of love that lives in you will light the way. Do not be afraid to shine it and you will not get lost in the darkness on the passage back.

The warrior knows the way. The warrior trusts, shines Light of Love, goes back, always remaining grateful for that which is revealed.

The pain of tomorrow is rooted in yesterday. The promises of tomorrow are the gifts hidden in the pain and the wisdom and strength to use those gifts are hidden in the pain. Nothing lost can be reclaimed without looking where it was last left behind.

You are part of a golden thread in a woven tapestry…meant to provide beauty, inspiration and hope to a part of the world that only sees gray….a part of the world that moves no longer by music. For it has been forgotten that music is created by love, for love; not money or profit….but to uplift and propel the souls of people who forgot. Music is the Great Gift that carries away fear, doubt, struggle…the sound waves carry away negative energy IF it is created by love for love.

Every person is a song. If you try to silence their song, steal a piece of their song, you only silence and rob yourself of harmony. You will become a broken instrument.

A true warrior does not fight the world but stands to fight that which is within that fights the world. The enemy is never out there. It is never as it appears. It is always within and projected outward *with the purpose of letting you see.* The more afraid you are to let your light of love shine, the more the enemy within will appear outward. Only the light of love opens the Eye Within. Keeping it closed only propels the enemy within to appear, enabling you to ignore no longer.

Everyone has the Gift of Life. Everyone is the Gift of Song. Everyone can give the Gift of Love. The light in you is waiting to shine on the world.

Be not invisible, break open the shell. The walls built to protect the heart, lock in and enclose the fear. The walls keep out the Blessing, the Flow of all things good and right. The torchlight: Follow the torchlight to find home. Rhapsody awaits. The eagle approaches the Song in the West Wind—hope for all people.

Starve not the man in black, but grace with the color of Being that which is within you—the rainbow of light/life. The past does not have to define you but is to provide insight and enrichment. The torchlight burns. The life that dances in front of you is to the song in your heart.

CALL TO REMEMBRANCE

Live the song that emanates from your soul. Dance your dream of long ago. Be the heroine of your own story. Let not the way of your heart grow cold nor despair, but fly free with the wings of the Truth of your Being. Stretch out beyond what you know; what is in front of you. The time is near.

Sleep no more in the dark of your heart. Tug the dream threads of existence, for the sacred fire burns ages old and Time forgotten.

All that you have and all that you are is written, etched into the pages of tomorrow. You know this yet you forget. The Silent Weeping Ones wait. The path to healing lies in you; in words, prayers and ancient songs by ancient tongues.

Weep not for what today has brought you. You are not as lost as you think you are. Pull the threads you are a part of. The weave is part of you and you part of it. Balance and Harmony are within you and yours to have and create. If your song is not your dance and your dance not your dream, make them one.

Embrace the pain and travel into it. It is there for reasons your mind cannot fathom. To run from it or escape it only allows it to persist. Run towards it with love and acceptance, entering into its heart. There, you will find the source of it all. There, you will find you—the lost pieces of you. There, you will remember your connection with Creator.

When you live the magic that is in you, then you will inspire the world.

Creator is not here to make life comfortable *for* you, but rather is here *with* you to create a comfortable life…a life that is able to comfort…not only yourself but also to comfort all you touch. And this, do with each other. Sing it on the high mountains and live it in the valleys below. Rob no one of the Essence of You.

And this is the greater calling. It is the great undertaking of the Ages. Be silent no more. Be invisible no more.

Seek not for beauty, but know beauty is you. To deny that there is beauty in this world, in your personal world, is to deny you. It is to deny That Which Flows Through You.

The Heart of Truth knows no boundaries of darkness but seeks to light the way through the darkness. The darkness is not to be feared for it is what illuminates Light for others to see it. If all were light, then no one could see. All would be blind. All will be Light when all can finally see. Then the darkness will not be necessary.

Remember all that you now hold out of fear, is that which surely holds you. All that you see is the illusion. All that you do not yet see is what is. The realness in you, of you is that which you do not see. Reflections of now guide the way Home to your Heart of Truth and the Essence of your soul. The Remembering is what fuels your fire—the blue flaming inferno within. It is the source of Inner Truth—the Divine Truth of your being.

THE WORTH OF YOU

As the power of light washes over you, conceptualize peace. Shape the outcome of tomorrow by what seeds you plant and dream today. Withdraw from the now serves no one, only allows seeds of discontent to grow wild and untamed.

The journey sprawls before you, wide open. Trust the way of spirit and guidance. Not all that is appearing is all that there is. Worry not. All things serve to guide in the highest good of everyone. To see the splendor that awaits is freedom of mind and heart. Step through the gateway of opportunity for it is broad, expansive. Look beyond the doorway that stands in front of you...trust...the mountains that faith moves are those built within the heart and mind.

You are a light of grace...a being of song, not to be swallowed by despair. You are one with all Life as it rejuvenates effortlessly; flowing, rippling and spiraling...like a vibrant dance.

As the sunbeams kiss the water while the wind blows, causing it to ripple and the sparkle dance on the surface; the water does not know or realize how beautiful and inspiring it looks to those who watch and are captivated by the sight. The water only feels the rippling and the wind. It only knows it is being moved.

It is the same with you. And when movement comes from some unseen force, and the light of the Divine Truth of your being shines down, you are...to someone, somewhere...a captivating and inspiring sight! You may not know or even feel that way, but you can trust that this is occurring just the same. Once you trust, you can begin to act accordingly. For you are one with all things. It is in the breath you share with all Life around you.

In that moment, you are becoming. You are a light of hope. It is not whether you travel through and reach the end, but rather how you travel through. The first serves only the mind of self. The second serves all that you are, Creator, and the world around you. It is of greater importance to the journey ahead. The fire in you seeks to thrive and purify, leading to compassion. It is great medicine. Accomplishing this is the first task...set sights on the dream star...the wish within...the heart prayer...ever feeling, ever trusting its presence in reality...in now.

Let not mind-bend occur. Do not be distracted by the material physical world. But gather force of heart and spirit to reign over. You are not yet what you appear in your own eyes, but something greater still. It is the eyes of Creator, the eyes of Love, who see all that you truly are.

~Archangel Azrael~

Archangel Sariel

Channeled by
Dianne Frazier

ANGELIC VOICE

As we walk our path, we too wish for comfort from OUR own kind to strengthen us from the persecution and harshness of this world as we strive daily to bring forth our light to those in need~ Listen for their WHISPERS~

In that hour the highest Angel could not vie with the meanest child of Adam as a comforter of Jesus. Never did He feel so much a man as when He began to sink deeper into man's wickedness and woes.

Here then was a new sorrow, disguised even in His comfort. For not only did He crave comfort directly from His Father and yet must be content with an Angel's instead, but next to His Father's. He craved sympathy from His own kind, His own flesh and blood, His chosen men, and an utterly different comforter was given Him the while that the Apostles slept and waited... Yet, notwithstanding all this, the Angel's coming was a gracious boon from His Father.

For now there suddenly burst upon Jesus a vision of blessed peace. The devils were gone who had been tormenting Him. Oh, what a difference -- this gentle being, and just as strong as gentle, full of brightness and affection, all beaming with hope, and peace, reverence and sympathy. How sweet a visit, how welcome a comfort. Hope rose in His Heart, though we hardly dare say joy... If we would speak of perfect kindness, we call it angelic; or perfect peace, we call it heavenly.

Thus Heaven vouchsafed to Jesus an interval, however brief, of its own gentle kindness, deep peace and rest. The Angel strengthened Him and Our Redeemer received at least a passing comfort from this most affectionate and reverent herald of celestial peace. He merited our eternal thanks for comforting our Champion in the direst moment of His awful conflict.

Christ knew that the only comfort possible for Him was within the gift of men alone, that is to say, their willingness to suffer with Him. But when the Angel was come, and before he vanished away, our saddened Redeemer thanked him lovingly, very grateful for his affectionate ministry.

The beauty and love that we Angels see in each of you is in the light you emit. As your vibration rises, so does your brightness. These are weary times, many of you wonder how to keep going, when the negativity around you lowers your connection with your higher self, and you long to go home to a place where you are understood with no language spoken.

We, too, long to feel the freedom of flight, to look down over the beautiful green and blue energies with the warm sun on our backs. In the Sun is the great love energy that connects each creature, even the smallest of us to one another. We know in our hearts that if one suffers, so do we all. Honor is earned by reacting spiritually to every test put in our path. The dark energy gives the choice of one path, the light another.

Living in human form, trying to understand these conditions is a sacrificial path, one chosen by us. Service before Self our mantra helps us to march forward. As we remember the GREAT MASTER Jesus too grew weary. Were it not for Gabriel speaking to him, comforting him, his last moments would have been so much more unbearable.

Remember as we walk amongst the living, that each soul longs to grow but all at different rates. Find patience; persevere through this journey to whisper the perfect words of love, to activate the remembrances as planned. Our light will attract many of all kinds. We will see the light in the eyes of these beings and when our guard is down their true nature may overcome their need to ascend.

It matters not, as time is eternal, and their time to achieve the path we helped to create will be offered again and again until the being follows their higher self's true calling. Again, our time in these bodies is short. Do as much as you can for as many as you can until again you find your wings. Your release from this realm will give you time to reflect, to plan and again to return. You will experience every laugh, every hope, and every tear.

You are a chosen one. Use your gifts only for the betterment of the souls you touch. As your body aches, remember the glow in the child's face as they left behind their terror to become whole again in the light.

This is a great honor, Rescuer of Lost Souls. You are the balance of the LIGHT. Represent it well. Honor all, Serve all. You will soon feel the air lifting your wings upward to the place we call home.

You will receive a
WARRIOR'S WELCOME!

~Archangel Sariel~

Wendy's Angel

Channeled by
Wendy Wenderful

THE TRUTH, CONSEQUENCES AND THE END OF INJUSTICE

The truth of the matter is not every truth matters, but the truth that matters most is also the hardest to tell.

Simple truths don't really matter. If you don't like someone's sweater you don't have to tell them. Maybe your friend's pets aren't exactly for you? These "truths" are more like "point of view." In fact, it isn't it nicer to not tell these truths at all?

Then you get into an area of varying complicated stuff. Someone you don't know has something in their teeth? You think you know someone is wrong about something you .know you are right about and could affect an outcome. How about someone you think is involved in illegal activity. Do you tell or do you avoid a mistake and responsibility and just "mind your own business?" Or is it the other way around? Are you responsible for not saying anything?

Then there are cases like this, you KNOW someone is dying but still tell them everything will be ok. Or is it really hope in which there is no truth? Hope is a fantasy, action is reality.

THERE IS NO ANGER

Anger is a word we use for any combination of negative impact emotions. Resentment, hurt, sadness, loss, pain, frustration, worry, hopelessness, fear, anxiety, disappointment are some that I have identified in my own life that have appeared to others as anger. Your list may be different.

Once we break our "anger" down to the actual emotions involved we are able to work through the emotions step by step, creating our own solution for recovery and healing within ourselves.

When we label all these emotions anger, we are denying ourselves and those we are angry with or who may be angry with us, the opportunity to resolve whatever it is we are angry about because we are not dealing with the actual emotions involved.

Think about the last time you were angry. What were you feeling and thinking? By breaking it down and figuring it out you will begin to understand yourself -- and those you care for -- more deeply. You may just find a resolution comes more easily because through honesty with ourselves we can become honest with those we are angry with, and stop causing unnecessary hurt and more anger.

Peace, Love, Respect and Harmony.

IMAGINE THE LIGHT

Morning
A new day begun,
No need to turn and run,
Feel the sun on your face,
Take you away to another place,
Imagine walking on the shore,
Free of pain forever more,
Keep your mind free
For things you long to be,
You can make it real, friend,
I trust you till the very end,
Just allow the morning light,
To take away the darkness, of the night.

~Wendy's Angel~

Jenni's Angel

Channeled by
Jennifer Whidden Turlington

HOPE FROM SADNESS

Oh Beloved! Why is there sadness in your heart? Yes, I see it. It shines through your eyes. You try to hide the pain, but those who truly see, know that it is there.

Arise, my beautiful child, for I have given you blessings above all! Your adversity reflects my love. I use it for my glory. Do you not know how you have reflected me in your journey of your life? Do you not see the beauty of the pain?

Look deep inside yourself and you know that I am speaking the truth. Again I say, you are loved! What was broken and desolate, I will repair with the healing of My mighty hand. I will call you up to be blessed!

You are like the bright shining star that beacons others to me. Your purpose is not yet fulfilled; your heartache is not yet over. You still have more to suffer, but Lo! I am God and I will heal you, I will save you, and I will comfort you in the days to come.

In your grief, sorrow, and pain; I will be there. Hold on tight to the teachings of God. You ain't seen nothin' yet!

~Jenni's Angel~

Angels of the Violet Ray

Channeled by
Sharam Tiemann

CREATING YOUR HEAVEN ON EARTH

Through your breath go in contact with the breath of Mother Earth and you will feel that you are at one with the breath of Mother Earth. We are not separated from her. She is a similar living body as you are. Over the evolution of time she gave you the chance to experience yourself on her. But mankind used their power unwisely, changed a lot on her surface and took even more out of her without restoring any balance or giving back to her.

We are now in the time where Mother Earth is not allowing us any further change on her nor taking anything out of her. She is now in a huge transformation process to balance herself again. This is happening in combination with some natural catastrophes such as volcanic eruptions, earthquakes, fires, flooding etc.

What mankind is asking for is to transform with Mother Earth together and to use your wisdom more wisely. Your real wisdom is stored in your Heart Chakra, in your unconditional love, not in your mind. In connection with your heart, your love which is your light, you will discover that you are a divine being, a soul, experiencing yourself in a human body. If you start living your love, you light up more and more and you follow the impulses out of your heart you will realize that you are all one. There is no separation from Mother Earth or from anything or anybody else. The state you are in at this moment is your creation.

Now you have the chance to create a better world out of Love and Peace. We are able to support you in your changing process which is needed for everyone as the physical body, every single cell; your chakra system and your Aura have to digest more and more light.

We are messengers of God to bring the Divine will onto Earth. You do not have to be afraid of us. Now is the time to work together again and you are the connection between heaven and earth. Only you have forgotten who you really are: Divine beings.

Make contact deeply with your love in your heart, your light, to realize who you really are and start to create wisely. All knowledge is within you. Stop searching outside of you. Take more time for your inner view and follow from here. Start to manifest and to create out of your Heart Chakra, your unconditional love. Only you can create a better world!

Imagine only for a moment that you are at one with everyone and everything. When you fight or are angry with yourself, the other person is only a mirror for you and with this understanding you can start to transform and release the things you don't like in the other person, actually in yourself.

With whom do you want to fight with when you are all one?

Start to share your love with everybody especially seemingly your enemies. Start to love everything that you meet in your life and you will see the chance to expand more and more into your full potential, your full power, and your qualities and share this with each other for the best of all.

You can bring your Heaven onto the Earth, so that you create together Heaven on Earth. It starts with you. Yes, exactly you who is reading this message. Start searching in yourself, in your love. If it is difficult for you just find people who can support you and let your heart be your compass.

~Angels from the Violet Ray~

An Angel called Rose

Channeled by
Terri McNeely

HELPING ANGELS

I am from the Angelic Realm never having lived an earthly incarnation. I appear in the color green usually as that is the color of healing. I came to Terri when she placed a call upon the Spirit wind for extra help in her life. She has her regular Spirit Guides as you all do. But she needed this help and also needed me for the rest of her earthly incarnation, she knew this.

Terri, a single parent since her son was eight was struggling on many levels, physically, mentally, emotionally and especially financially. There had been so many times in her life she just wanted to totally give up. But she knew she couldn't. It was at this point that she had placed her call for the highest help available to hang in there, to fight the odds and to keep going. Her Soul lessons of this life have been hard and she does continue to learn them and go to the next lesson.

I am also her creative muse whether she is making jewelry, playing guitar, singing whatever she chooses to do at the moment.

Those of us from the Angelic Realm are always available for help for any and all who need us. There are Angels who come to you when you call for a certain task. When that is completed, you may not need us anymore so we move on to another. We will always stay with you for as long as you need us.

You have to ask for this help for on your plane of existence there is Free Will. We are not allowed to intervene unless we have your permission, though we are right there until you do ask. When you move to another task, a new Angel is available to you to bring you farther along.

So, whatever you need whether it is for your lifetime or just a short time, please call upon us. We wish to help any and all for whatever that reason is. Please understand that we want to help you whether your need is small or large. We enjoy this and want you not to fear that you are taking our time away from maybe another being. That is not the case! So fear not in asking. There are plenty of us here in this realm for any or all needs at anytime whether short or lifetime.

Thank you for allowing me to share with you. It has been my extreme pleasure. I hope that I have conveyed that we are here for you in anyway and anytime. I send you all my highest Blessings and Love!

~Rose~

Archangel Azrael

Channeled by
Daena Croghan

ANGELIC SUPPORT

To those who don't know me, allow me to introduce myself. I am the angel of Death. Fear not as I am the one who escorts you to the other side of life when it is time. You will see my face or the face of one of my descendents the exact moment you die. I have a team of angels whose allegiance is purely to God and our purpose. We work in silence, without reward, to ensure that all humans cross over safely to their destination.

What is our purpose shall you ask? It is an answer that cannot be answered lightly. I will attempt to explain to you why you humans are so important to beings/angels that have capacity far beyond your own.

You are our creation. Each human heart is directly connected to that of an angel. Angel is a word that describes many types of beings but we will use it here for lack of a better pronoun. In this sense we will just say that an angel is a being that is greater than human. By terming ourselves greater, we do not mean that we are better than or more important. We mean that we have infinite power and resources at our fingertips and know how to use it. Humans have all the power and resources but haven't the slightest clue how to access it regularly. We find you especially interesting, lovable, quirky, amusing and worthy as you remind us so much of ourselves.

There is so much to be learned from angel-human interactions. We learn from you more than you learn from us. That is not to say that we don't try to help and offer our guidance. Some humans can be very stubborn and not accepting of our help. Though our hearts are connected, if a human does not want us, we do not force ourselves upon them. We wait, patiently, for them to open and summon us.

Once a human does open to an angelic presence, the relationship unfolds and is more powerful than any human to human connection. Your technology was created to merge with that of the higher realms and we know just how to administer since we are your makers.

I speak of myself as "we" more so than "I" because our angelic force has accepted that all souls are one. It's hard to speak only of myself because I cannot see myself without seeing everyone else. We are slowly working with the Earth plane and bringing that awareness to all cultures and religions. Soon there will be no separation between the heavenly dimensions and Earth. We are working to make ourselves better known and more visible to more humans all the time.

There will come a time where all beings will be able to coexist and thrive in harmony together under full acceptance of God. Until then, all humans will continue to receive energy attunements, soul regeneration, and physical enhancements from the angelic realm to better prepare for this phase of merging. The merging process won't be long once it starts and in just a few lifetimes from now, all beings will be able to know each other and communicate with each other. Perceived darkness is only that which is unknown. Merging all consciousness together will take care of any unknowingness and will only leave pure acceptance, faith, and love.

This magically brightens our hearts with the excitement of being able to make ourselves known to your kind. We have awaited this day for centuries. This long distance communication we are experiencing now will soon be over and so will a huge part of human suffering. The Earth can return to her function of supporting the life that she sustains, in harmony and peace.

With this new hope, please keep in mind that though this merging brings good things, some humans will do everything they can to resist. It is our job to love them unconditionally and help them gently through their suffering. We ask of you humans to assist us with bringing every sentient being to their readiness in every way that you can. Feed the hungry, clothe the poor, hold the hand of a scared child, be patient and kind to the elderly. All of these things and more are the quality of an angel. If you see yourself displaying these behaviors already, please continue for we angels can use all the help we can get.

Call on us and we will be there. There are no boundaries that keep us from you except for you. Please know that we want only for humans to rise above their conflict and suffering and reach their true potential. We know that it's possible and are working to make it happen. Every time you see a flash a bright light or sense a presence near you, do not be frightened as it is your angel.

Until we meet again,

~Azrael~

Various Archangels

Channeled by
Amanda Dowling

MESSAGES OF HOPE

Archangel Michael
I come to you to remind you that I have compassion for humanity. With the sword of protection I teach you to cut away the cords that no longer serve you. When you give me permission, I stand with my sword and cut away any negative energy blocks or cords that no longer serve us through our journey. I ask that you remember your function on this earth as a creator of life, which was created from a main source called Father- Mother God or Creator.

When this happens if we can remind ourselves to cancel, clear and delete that which does not serve us. We are instantly changing what is around us...reminding you that you can change the circumstances in a situation which you do not enjoy being in. Your choices are to remain where you are or move forward. That is what life is like for today's world. You are learning about this.

Now that we are on the subject of shifting energy, many of you are aware of 2012 and the ending of the earth which has been predicted. This, I come to reassure you, is a prediction. We can change this prediction as we can change the circumstances we are living right now. The choice is up to you. I remind you of this just like you call upon me for help in vacuuming out that which is cobwebs of energy in your system of chakras or you ask to cut cords to people and situations that do not serve you.

2012 is not the end of the world unless everyone decides to not work together as a team to come from love and light. 2012 is our beginning to release the old patterns that do not serve this planet anymore, to cut away the old energy, to embrace a new energy that will come in to connect all of humanity into unconditional love energy. The choice is up to you on this.

You must decide to come together no matter what race or religion or what state or country you are from, to embrace the energy of light and healing or to continue in a ruling light of pressure. We are at war with one another and at war with the energy which is of lower vibrational quality. You can choose to come into the new vibrational energy of oneness and consciousness.

I am here to remind you that all of humanity is connected to the earth no matter where you live, what food you eat, what country you live in and what color you are. We are all energy of a source called creator or Father Mother God and it is up to you as a connected planet to come back together without fighting and being in competition.

This is a time to help out your neighbor and encourage one another in light and healing. I encourage you to invite the frequency of unconditional love into your presence today.

Archangel Raphael

I come to you to remind you this is a time of great need to heal. Many of us are wounded and in fear. We are at war with one another with much bloodshed at this time. You were brought here with many different walks of life and each journey is different. You have learned about war and the lower vibrations of greed and of untruth and also of competition. Now is the time to embrace the healing.

Many of you are afraid of the word 2012. What does it stand for? Well, some say the end of your planet that you live on and the end of life. This is stated to wake you up about your planet. Your planet is a living being, just as you are, and very wounded. Mother Earth cries for help and asks you to stop with the wars, greed, judgment, greediness, control, war, completion, anger, hate. Instead, come together out of love.

Right now you are being shown that each of you come from the same place. This place that you dwell is alive and has feelings. You have polluted her and also had war and many other things that you have had Earth mother take on. Now she is tired and is having to work hard to release and cleanse all of the damage. You are being asked to come together and help her heal so that this place is one to live on with love.

As she cleanses there are natural disasters earthquakes, tornados, tsunamis and more. This means that Mother Earth is cleaning house and cleansing herself and asking that there are no more wounds that we come together in healing and help one another. This is a time for peace and not war; a time where people come together just as family, even if you are friends, to just heal and support one another out of a community.

My message to you is stop fighting and being in fear of 2012, and start taking a stand for healing. You are not alone in these times of despair, loneliness, sadness and more. I am here with you to help you to heal and recover from the circumstances that are traumatizing. I am here to bring light and healing to everyone on this planet while surrounding you with love and light.

Archangel Alexander

My name is Alexander the Archangel and I am here to tell you that in these times of loss, if you feel lost just call on any of us. We are here to send you much comfort and light. Whether you are worried about your loved ones, job, finances, the world or your family, all of the angels are here to assist you.

You can tell us any of your worries and we can carry a bucket to you and you can place this in our bucket for us to carry and take up to the sky for you. You can also write to us so that you feel we can hear you. Some of you even enjoy burning the piece of paper to send this to the sky. Whether you are manifesting to the universe or talking to us -- any preference of communication you prefer -- we get the message. The important thing to remember is to pray and give us permission to help you.

We love talking with you through songs on the radio, signs like feathers, books, touching your shoulder, giving you a dream, talking to you in your ear, even just showing up to you, but we do this in the gentlest form.

We are not here to harm you but want you to know that you can talk to us any way you want and the call is free. And you do not even need a telephone. We are always listening for your calls for help and your talks that you have with us. We love talking with you too.

Archangel Gabriel

In this time the message I have for you is to listen to the clear communication I am giving you that right now you are shifting on the planet earth. This means you may receive all kind of communication from us…through writing, songs, dreams, books, whispers in the ear, through your daily life of people. Just look around you at the signs of hope and you will see that there is communication being made between you and any of us. This is a time of healing and peace right now. You are in trying times where you need words of faith. This is the time to come together and support one another. Do not act out in war and in fear but come from a place of love and light. .

Archangel Uriel

My name means justice and fire of God. At this time we are burning up any old ways that do not serve us. My job is to burn up these old ways that do not work for you here on earth, and to supply you with new universal laws.

These laws are Father Mother God's laws which tell us we will be coming from a place of light not a place of fear and lower frequency. Right now the challenge is staying close to the light. Remember that what you put out to the world, you will get back. So if you put out negativity, you will receive negativity back. At this time it is important to stay in a loving space, to not create that which is lower vibration. To live your life like it is a prayer.

Archangel Metatron
   My name is Metatron, healer and guide of shapes. As we shift, we are in a time of need with prayers. We can remember to pull up the earth energy from the ground and also the sky energy from source Father-Mother God. This is important to stay grounded. When you are pulling up this energy you can imagine a pyramid facing up and a pyramid facing down and surround yourself in a circle. This will help you stay centered.

An Angel called Az

Channeled by
Tim Tedana

ACTIONS ARE TRUTH

No soul can be redeemed by another soul or soul groups with hierarchies and oaths of sacred obedience. Knowledge is not "Wisdom." No Saints, Angels nor even God(s), have the ability to shield an evolving soul from the consequences of its own karmic doings. We truly "reap what we sow". Everyone must eventually become their own saviors. Not simply by speaking the words of "love all, serve all," but by becoming the living 'word' for all to see and emulate. Behind the invisible veil, the hosts of both realms take note. Words are cheap, but ones actions - tell all.

TRUE LOVE

True love is an unconditional energy. It is beautiful when it is given freely between two souls. To experience it even for just a moment; angels would, and have willingly ... fallen. If you love someone and your depth speaks to the other - you have a meeting in spirit; it is a breathtaking experience.

However, if it is not happening and the energy is instead, one of pain - separate. But do not create any conflict, struggle or fight for it, because it cannot be achieved through battle, and precious time is lost - not only time, but your capacity to truly love will also be damaged. If you are there only for security, you will not find it. If you are jealous you will not find it, if you are there simply for sex, again ...you will not find this intangible magic called love.

If there is no trust, separate - the sooner, the better. So that you are not destroyed, so that you are not damaged, so that your capacity to love remains unscathed so that you can someday love somebody else.

Trust cannot be forced. If there is no trust simply acknowledge; this is not the place, this is not the man or woman for you and move on. But do not destroy each other. There is no need to determine a villain.

Understand, not all souls are on the same level of evolution. Not all energies are meant to be compatible. When love exists between two souls, there exists a trust that he/she will not go to anybody else, will not give themselves to another.

If he/she does, then in reality there was no true love to begin with and nothing can be done. Loves brings this understanding between two souls and with it, trust.

True love is an unconditional energy. It is beautiful when it is given freely between two souls.

To experience it even for just a moment; angels would, and have willingly ~ fallen.

THE ANGELS PATH

Living ethereal shadows beam with unearthly glows. Ancient entities that have seen all; experienced all that humanity is capable of first hand. At one time both were worshipped in history as Gods and cursed as Demons. They are neither, and they love unconditionally.

Always do they respond when called upon by the newest children of the Gods. Every so often one can one can hear their subtle whispers, one can feel their presence if one truly stills one's mind and listens with ones heart and soul. They do not answer prayers; they are neither Gods nor the proverbial tooth fairies of the divine realms.

They will however, help humans find truths and ways to answer their own desires if they truly wish to experience the wonders and mysteries of life. From antiquity to present;

embodied or in spirit, regardless of the form taken, they remember why they are here; to help guide and protect, until the last new souls evolve on to higher realms.

SERVANTS OF THE STARS

Humans are magical creatures. Within them they have direct links; divinity within to the divine without. If only they realized how truly great they are. The power to create, given unto them. Their dreams and perceptions affecting not just their own realities, but all those near them as well.

All are here to play in this experimental collective "free-will" zone within this universe. Your dreams and thoughts can change this world into one of light or dark. Choice is the rule here. Your dreams are blueprints of creation that affect events; not just within this world, but in many unseen as well. It is why the stars themselves watch with great interest.

The only limits of these magical creatures are those they place upon themselves by their beliefs. Every human soul in every culture and path is a direct child of the Gods. Servants of the stars are always near. Not to save them from their created realities, but simply to assist and guide when called upon.

Quiet your mind of all thoughts, and you will hear their whispers within. All have the ability to summon assistance from worlds unseen. Inherited within all divine human souls, the ability of their parents to create or destroy.

Your collective dreams create worlds and realities. So my friends, dream as only angels can.

TRANSFORMATIONS

Allow yourself to take a journey with me to an isolated back yard jungle. A private hide- away with secluded benches where one can take a breath from civilization and let nature speak to you in its own subtle way. Within this wild garden/jungle float about many beautiful, colorful winged creatures.

They did not begin life that way. Watch with me as they float by immersed in their own unique world. Does the caterpillar know what is in store for him or her when they spin themselves into the darkness? Are they afraid to enter that dark realm? No, I think not.

For they have no religious dogma dictating fear. The transformation required elements of dark and light. In accepting nature's laws and cycles…they evolve.

What tells them it is time to stop being who they are and become something else, to become something beyond their wildest dreams and desires? When they emerge from the dark, are they hesitant to stretch their wings and take flight into the light of day? Are they afraid of that first leap of faith?

Their transformations do make the world such a nicer place, yes? Their simple presence, affecting so many without even being aware of the magic they bring with them.

When we are young, we have many fantasies and dreams. Everything is possible. All through our lives, we are faced with opportunities to make decisions, to change and to grow. As we mature, we are taught to distinguish between fantasies and what is considered real, between the possible and the impossible. Humanity slowly loses that essence that made everything magical and possible.

Sometimes, humans simply follow paths and beliefs because everyone else states that is what they should do as a responsible 'adult' in any given particular society. They turn away from their own assumptions and beliefs, their own inner lights which make everything possible. Fears surface and dictate all actions and color all thoughts.

Fears of the unknown are involved with self-discovery, as well keeping them trapped forever within their own self-imposed cocoons. This prevents the magical entities within from spreading their wings and being all that they are capable of - beautiful, colorful winged creatures.

Simply food for thought.

CREATE YOUR REALITY

Conflict rages within...Indecisions...Such markers in life occur for specific purposes - that is the way of this realm. The availability of choice is not a curse. It is a blessing. It is empowerment. You do not face your trials alone, though it often feels as such. Ones such as you have been blessed with knowledge from higher realms when facing trials as you now do. You have the gift of foresight. Many in life do not. Never do most realize that they themselves chose and created their own realities.

Many see themselves as victims of circumstance, when in truth they are not. You contain so much knowledge. Knowledge enables you to recognize the subtle signs that have such a great impact on our directions in life. Most do not see choice; do not understand that they and only they are responsible for the experiences they are living. When one sees a middle-aged person living in an alley, all the observer sees is that individual at a specific point in time. They do not see the hundreds upon hundreds of choices that the individual made that caused them to be where they are now.

All create their own worlds. That is the saving grace, the innate beauty that lies just beneath the surface of this apparent dark chaotic realm. You must first decide what it is you wish to experience, envision your ideal life. If you wish, peace, love and joy. Then ask yourself questions, and let you heart answer them. You have many who care for you. When your mind cannot give you the answers to your questions, then look deeper within. Listen then to the emotions emanating from within your heart, for emotions are the language of the soul.

As an exercise, close your eyes for a few minutes and feel for the energy within you that is you. Then say to yourself softly, "I love the direction my government is directing this nation."

Without speaking, feel the response in your heart, feel the emotion. That response is the true answer your soul is giving you. Now say softly, "I love my father deeply, and miss him." Listen and feel for the response within.

Your soul gave you true answers in both cases. It is that easy. Feelings are the language of the soul. It is the way. White Feather taught me to know the true path.

My quote to live by: "I shall be telling this with a sigh somewhere ages and ages hence: Two roads diverged in the woods, and I -- I took the one less traveled by, And that has made all the difference." ~ Robert Frost~

This journey has been a long and hard one. You see darkness all around you. You want happiness, joy, peace, serenity. You cry out to the universe and it responds. Its answer is similar to what Glenda, the Good Witch of the North said to Dorothy at the end of that long hard adventure she believed she had to undertake to make her wish come true..

"..Why, my dear - you have had the power to grant your own wishes, all along."

You are blessed. Know this to be an absolute truth. You are loved by many. Regardless of what your choices may be this life, you always will be...

I am frequently asked, for some odd reason, on the nature of this realm, life, time, how and why? Perhaps many wish the view from one who is not grounded here well and thinks outside of the circle?

I always urge all souls to learn and study for themselves. I will suggest topics to read if they ask. But I like for them to come to their own conclusions. Despite that, many still wonder why I do not worry that the 'end' of the world may be approaching.

There are many prophecies of doom and gloom from many theological paths, both from the present and the past. I smile; I view the "game" differently, without a doubt. Understand that no life is permanent. Look at the many cemeteries that exist, now and in ancient times. Still, many like to ask. Usually the same questions from many.

I hope this helps with questions pertaining to time and the 'end of the world'. Or even the end of the known universe for that matter. Keep in mind; this is from the perspective of one - not of the light, nor of the dark. Let us call it from a neutral observer's perspective - one who simply watches.

Let us diverge for a moment, from human reality to that of universal spiritual aspects of energy and 'how' the stage occurs. All energies; light and dark (dark matter as it is now called) have intelligence. Know this. We are the universe made conscious to experience itself.

Let us take a brief (very brief) synopsis of 'how' the universe (stages or realms) that are perceived here and work from beginning to end. Let us delve into the mechanics behind this, in a nutshell.

Keep in mind; this is my story only, my spin on what I lovingly call the game. One must look within to find truth. All I say, you will doubt until you do discover for yourself. Hence begin studying as I always recommend. And if by chance after much in-depth analytical searching you find another reality, I will simply smile at the soul within you. We are after all, long time friends.

The world and universe as we know it has ended as many have envision it....many, many (many) times. It is a game that never ends. Many seers in what is now called 'history' simply remember bits and pieces called 'visions' and printed their visions in ancient text.

But do not fear, though each 'life' or game is temporary; know we are embodied universal energy. We are eternal. You are guaranteed to experience 'life' while you accomplish your path. Whether a soul light or dark, human or watcher, that soul chooses to sit in a bunker for a 'life' (regardless of it duration) watch grass grow, or wishes to walk out and interact and partake in all life has to offer, it is all up to that soul.

I would advise to continue your chosen path while living life, but that is up to you. All --regardless of status -- have choice. When one of my fragments, Tim, was in his 20's, he gave no thought to his inner-self. He simply lived. He was simply happy that he no longer saw the dead walking or heard them speaking as he did when he was a child until his young teens. He saw other things as well, that were not of this realm. But, finally when in his 20's he was 'normal.' He was simply relieved, to have lost the 'sight'. He just wanted to be human. He did not even activate again on the path until his 30's.

I reminisce of many things, like most. That is one of the joys in life. But I also realize that everything I surround myself with now is ultimately nothing but stardust in a cosmic wind. Each game is temporary, and life has no guarantees. Simply the pursuit of happiness and adventure is what you are allowed. Yet each life and adventure is unique from its perspective and because of this, each life is sacred.

Many are scientific minded, yes? Good, instead of looking at this purely from a spiritual aspect. Let us also look at it from a science aspect as well.

We know from a religious aspect and science that in the beginning there was nothing. Then 'they' said "Let there be light." And, like 'magic', it was suddenly there. From a science aspect you have the Big 'Bang' Theory. They are much the same really. There was nothing. Then there was something. Actually the same event but the story is simply told from two different perspectives, yes?

You all know of 'Time' as outlined by Albert Einstein? Curvature and the speeding and slowing of time as it relates to ripples in the fabric of space and gravity? You know of the premise outlined in Quantum psychics? Quantum reality with Einstein's explains a bit of the mechanisms of the spirit world and the three dimensional world that you perceive as real. Not the reasons; simply the mechanics. Learn those two if you are not versed on them.

Knowledge is everything, my dears. A teacher you seek to be, then knowledge you must as well know. Anyway, known to humans presently, the big bang existed because, in computer generated models, a map exists showing galaxies are moving away from each other at a very, very fast rate. Like a shotgun shell leaving a barrel. The projected paths of travel by the galaxies, when put in reverse, indicate that all universes/galaxies began at a single point in time and space. An explosion of epic proportions occurred where only darkness once appeared to exist. Like a massive black hole of unheard of proportions, spewing out all of its energy at one time to create what we now call our universe and eventually - *life*.

The center of this 'energy' of dark still exists. Actually, part of it is centered in every galaxy, regulating and observing the game. Its consciousness is all around us. The rate of the expanding light (star clusters, galaxies), created by the dark continues to spread outward at the speed of light through time in a cosmic blink of an eye. As they grow and spread, 'life' as humans know it begins to unfold. Thousands upon thousands of planets separated by space now play hosts to many 'games' all at once.

In reference to all that is known, please do not think in linear terms. All things exist as a circle. No star or light (which is what galaxies are created of) burns forever. They all will eventually die out. This is proven by human science (as limited as it is at this juncture). But while light exists, is it not a beautiful thing to behold and be? Where was I?

Oh yes, when Stars die they revert to what they once were, humans refer to them as huge dark holes in space. They take in energy yes, but are in themselves very much a different type of energy with consciousness. Once again remember all energy has consciousness.

Let us return back to the model of life, the mechanics of the 'game' shall we? Let's see… oh yes, time continues on. Billions of stars of light that helped to create the millions of games or realities are now fading, returning energy to what it once was.

As the path of billions of now 'apparent' fading and deceased stars, dark energies or holes continue on the journey. They will begin to head back towards each other.

Think of the path the energy follows, not as a straight line, but instead think of the surface of a ball or a circle. The energy of light starts on one end and spreads from that point to all directions on this ball. It travels along the surface of the circle (for discussions sake again, a ball). As it crosses the midpoint, the once myriad of many lights begins to fade. The millions upon millions of dots of light become as they once were...dark. The energies, now well past the horizon of the curved ball's surface, head towards each other on the other end at tremendous speed.

Once again, however, there is not one speck of light left. There appears to be nothing, only darkness. The millions and millions of Dark Holes & Dark galaxies contained in them combine the living consciousness of all that ever was from all perspectives of embodied light and dark. The million components of energy larger than one can fathom, eventually collide, merging into one great living mass of pure living energy.

The force and power of such a union is so immense and wonderful that time and space ceases to be. All knowledge is again shared by all. All experiences, shared by all. For a brief moment that lasts forever... all are "one". To the eye (if someone were to observe all from a distance) nothing but a dark void would seem to exist. But an empty void, it is not.

When such energy meets and merges lessons of all that was...are reviewed.

Experiences, moments from all are relived and examined. Time and Space cease to be. Once done, The "ALL" again seeks an adventure. 'We' chose to again, set the stages to 'be'. We decide again, create the adventures we crave and love so much. We again say, "Let there be light."

An explosion again occurs in a flash of brilliant light. Millions of galaxies composed of light, are again born in an instant. Emerging from what appears to be a dark void of nothingness, going in the opposite direction from the point of apparent creation. It begins to spread out into the cosmos over the horizon again at the speed of light.

The 'game' in this realm again begins. A game that never ends. The consciousness of you never ceases to be. Simply your perspectives change. Your roles change. A new universe from *appearances* is created. Embodied souls may again enjoy the illusion of life, of loss, of death and birth, of being alone and finding the one elusive great love that makes life seem complete. They test themselves again and again in the great game.

One may walk away from your chosen path any time you wish. That is choice. You chose a path, you may change it. Simply knowing the mechanics behind the game does not mean the ride is any less exciting. It simply means you have knowledge of what makes the roller coaster work.

You are presently in a hologram type existence. You are both teacher and student within a living history lesson. While we are here we are being watched by, for lack of a better term, a school board of sorts, or a Council, to insure the curriculum and rules of engagement are followed.

You are also given help by angels, or counselors or guides as some prefer to call them - should you need assistance on your path to meet your goals.

You have a body. You have gifts; some will play the role of seers with visions and knowledge, but can't remember why. But all have some sort of gift(s) to help them on their chosen paths. What the players chose to do with their gifts is up to them. There is choice in all things. Their actions define what they are within to those that watch behind the invisible veil. If you are in the game, the basic rules apply.

Simply having some knowledge of the mechanics behind the illusion of the game will not change the course of the game. How you play the game is all that matters. Find adventure, find your great love. A chance again to be what you wish or experience this life. That 'chance' is the only thing promised.

That is what makes the game exciting -- this wonderful three-dimensional reality as you know it.

Be light and love if that is what you chose, and enjoy the game for what it is - simply an adventure for your soul.

May there always be angels to help light your way through your many journeys my dear friend.

~ Az ~

PROTECTION, HEALING AND CLEARING MEDITATION

Archangel Anael gave me a Pyramid Protection Modality to share with the world. It is recorded on a 22 minute CD or mp3 download which can be purchased on my website. www.morganastarr.com

However, the shortened version I have included here is very powerful. After bringing in this energy, you simply must think of it three times a day. Take a deep breath in and a deep breath out while visualizing the pyramid firmly in your mind. Do this for three breaths seeing the pyramid of light go around you each time, so you have three layers thick.

This is especially helpful for Light workers and awakening empaths. An empath is someone that is highly sensitive and may get overwhelmed in large crowds. An empath feels others emotional pains. This can exhibit as fatigue, depression and eventually physical pain.

Say it aloud with feeling, knowing as you speak it is created with the help of the angels.

"Archangel Anael, please create a Divine pyramid of protection around me. The top of the pyramid is connected to the heart of the Divine where there is a valve leading inwards only. At the bottom in each corner are valves leading outwards only. Anything touching the bottom of the pyramid is instantly transmuted into love…siphoned to the corner valves sent into Mother Earth to balance and heal her.

It fills my pyramid, filtering through my body taking any negativity, worries or imbalances. This goes to the bottom of my pyramid being instantly transmuted into Love, through the valves to balance and heal Mother Earth.

Anael, please manifest a rainbow through my pyramid and through my body, balancing and healing each chakra. Please fill my pyramid with tiny rainbows full of joy!

Anything negative that brushes the sides of my pyramid and is instantly transmuted into love, great health and prosperity on every level for me.

Please cloak the outside of my pyramid, so darkness will not perceive my Light as I shine brighter and brighter on my Divine Path.

Anael, please keep the pyramid and rainbows with me always. Thank You, Anael for your help and assistance."

FINAL WORDS FROM ANAEL

Winds of change blow across your face bringing promises of new beginnings. The angels wing their way to your side. The area around you fills with the heavenly hosts. They tell you that because you believe in them, they believe in you. As you breathe, they breathe new life into you. The dreams that you have had, you have outgrown. Your reality will become better than you could ever have imagined!

An angel's wings know no limits as they can fill the sky with their very essence. They can traverse the globe and even the universe. They will take you to the places you need to go and will bring to you the people you need in your life.

You are the true 'Warriors of the Rainbow'. Use the energy of the Rainbow to heal yourself first. Protect and clear and heal yourself with each breath as you invoke my Pyramid of Light over you. Then you will find that as the world is healed we are all One. That is ... true 'Warrior' work.

~Archangel Anael~

ABOUT THE AUTHOR

Reverend Morgana Starr is a Psychic Medium, Spiritual Adviser, Reiki Master/Teacher, Facilitator for The Melchizedek Method of Healing (Sacred Geometry), Angel Messenger, a Native American Pipe Carrier, and Florida Paranormal Research Foundation Psychic Medium .

Morgana has been following a healing path for most of her life. A child of missionary parents in Africa, she was raised in the Christian Church. From their isolated mission site to the Prime Minister's home for tea her formative years in Africa were rich and varied. When they returned to America, she went from living at a Church camp to Bible College to marriage and children.

Not satisfied with the confines of traditional religion, in the 1990's Morgana began a search to find deeper spiritually in order to enhance her relationship with the Divine. Morgana then received her Reiki training, which reawakened psychic gifts from childhood.

At this point people whom had passed on began talking to her, as well as she began to receive psychic (prophetic) messages. She remembered the words of Jesus, "These things I do, you too will do and more," Therefore she dedicated her gifts to the Divine and always kept herself surrounded by the Divine White Light.

So she let go of control and allowed the Divine to take her spiritual gifts to a higher level. She continued taking more intense spiritual training in different modalities, in Colorado, New Mexico, Ohio, Indiana and California.

This gives her a diverse background of spirituality to draw upon to help her clients. She has used her gifts to connect many people with their loved ones whom have passed on. Her ability to tune into a person's totem animal or guardian angel assists her in teaching her clients how to tap into their own power and energy for the betterment of their own health and happiness.

Anael had been working with Morgana all of her life, though in a subtle, unconscious way. April of 2008, she was living in Indiana, Anael manifested clearly and assisted her to walk away from her last disempowering relationship and most of her belongings and fly to Florida.

She teaches Psychic Development Classes in the Cocoa Beach area of Florida. She also offers personalized classes and session via the internet and the phone.

Morgana helps people with:

Daily Grief or Depression, Emotional and relationship issues, Pain management, Stress Relief, Past Life Regression, Psychic Blueprint Reading, Energy Balancing, Spiritual Healing

Morgana's writing credits include publication in *Branches* and *Horizons* magazines. She has several Meditation CDs available to help you on your spiritual path.

You can contact Morgana directly through her website: www.morganastarr.com

She would love to hear from you!

CONTRIBUTING AUTHORS

ANGELIC ENCOUNTERS

ANGELS WALK AMONG US
Submitted by: Reverend Beverly Hale Watson
Founder/Director of Sevenfold Peace Foundation and Author
BHWDove@Verizon.net,
www.eclectusville.com/Angel_Times_1.html

ANGEL MECHANICS
Submitted by: Donna Hunter

DAD'S ANGEL
Submitted by: Cynthia Abruzzo DeSiena
Owner of Heavenly Bake Shoppe
www.heavenlybakeshoppe.com

HOSPITAL ANGEL
Submitted by: Katherine Kovacs

SURGEON'S ANGEL
Submitted by: Andrea de Michaelis
Psychic/Medium, Publisher and Owner of Horizons Magazine,
Spiritual Solutions for Florida Since 1992
www.horizonsmagazine.com

ANGEL DOODLING MESSAGE, GUARDIAN LAUNDRY
ANGEL
Submitted by: Marita VanSmoorenburg Shaffer

SHIELDING WITH ANGEL LOVE
Submitted by: Misty Dawn, LMT

Psychic/Medium, Spiritual Healer, Reiki Master/Teacher
www.radiantspirit.com

ANGEL DRAGONS
Submitted by: Susan Solivan, LMT
Massage Therapist, Psychic Medium, Spiritual Healer
www.craniosacral-susan.com, www.michaelsheateaching.com

MESSAGES FROM ANGELS

THE PATH, THIS TOO WILL PASS
An Angel called White Feather
Channeled by: Lisa Johnston-Anderson

ANGELIC LOVE
Shandie's Angel
Channeled by: Shandie Savage
Artistic Designer of Anael's symbol
psychekitty@yahoo.com
www.facebook.com/shandie.savage

LOVE YOURSELF AS MUCH AS I LOVE YOU,
YOUR DREAMS ARE WHAT BROUGHT YOU HEAR
Cynthia's Angel
Channeled by: Cynthia Segal
Intuitive Consultant, Medium, Featured in the Award Winning Inspirational Documentary movie "Real People, Real Shifts"
www.CynthiaSegal.com

CALL TO RELEASE, CALL TO EXPLORATION, CALL TO ACTION, CALL TO REMEMBRANCE, THE WORTH OF YOU
Archangel Azrael
Channeled by: Rebecca Ausband Snavely, LMT
Spiritual Healer, Massage Therapist
www.triessencemassage.com

ANGELIC VOICE
Archangel Sariel
Channeled by: Dianne Frazier
Psychic/Medium
www.diannespiritlight.com

THE TRUTH, CONSEQUENCES AND THE END OF INJUSTICE, THERE IS NO ANGER, IMAGINE THE LIGHT
Wendy's Angel
Channeled by: Wendy Wenderful
Rainbow Free Spirit Energy
www.artofbeing.imagekind.com,
www.everythingiswenderful.blogspot.com

HOPE FROM SADNESS
Jenni's Angel
Channeled by: Jennifer Whidden Turlington
Attitude of Gratitude Project
www.facebook.com/aogp.org

CREATING YOUR HEAVEN ON EARTH
Angels from Violet Ray
Channeled by: Sharam Tiemann
Angel Messenger, Spiritual teacher, Healer & Artist
Angels of Light Centre Edinburgh/Scotland
www.aolc.co.uk

HELPING ANGELS from An Angel called Rose
Channeled by: Terri McNeely
Psychic Medium, Reiki Master Teacher, Owner of Owl Visions
www.smile-village.com/OwlVisions

ANGELIC SUPPORT from Archangel Azrael
Channeled by: Daena Croghan
Psychic Medium, Spiritual Healer, Reiki Master

MESSAGES OF HOPE from Various Archangels
Channeled by: Amanda Dowling
Psychic Medium, Spiritual Healer, Angel Messenger
www.ancestoroflight.webs.com

ACTIONS ARE TRUTH, TRUE LOVE, SERVANTS OF THE STARS, TRANSFORMATIONS, CREATE YOUR WORLD
from An Angel named Az
Channeled by: Tim Tedana
Director of Florida Paranormal Research Foundation
www.floridaparanormal.com

CPSIA information can be obtained at www.ICGtesting.com
Printed in the USA
LVOW090250031011

248819LV00002B/9/P

9 781614 345244